The Winning Edge

The Student-Athlete's
Guide to College Sports

Second Edition

by

Frances and James Killpatrick

Contents

Acknowledgements

We would like to thank all the athletic directors, sports information directors and their staffs, high school guidance counselors and coaches, college admissions people, student-athletes and their parents who shared their valuable information and experience with us. Without them, this book could not have been written. Our special thanks go to the leading coaches who provided their constructive insights into taking your sport to college.

For their guidance and support, we are particularly indebted to: Catharine Alexander, Karen Bizier, Sandra Brent, Hildegarde Carlyle, Charles Cavagnaro, Bill Dobson, Chrissie Edmundson, Stewart Faught, Anna Griswold, Cecil Hart, Jeff, Anne and Jordan Irving, Bill Kilpatrick, Randy Lambert, Scott Lindley, Dan Meier, Mike Mullan, Ruth Perlstein, Kitty Porterfield, Marcia Saneholtz, The Rev. Robert Sunderland, S.J., and Andrew Wiederhorn.

And last, but definitely not least, thanks to our grown children, Amy and Pat, whose perceptive reading of the manuscript helped keep us in line.

Cover design by Supon Design Group.
Typesetting by Edington-Rand Inc.

Address Correspondence to:

Octameron Associates, Inc.
P.O. Box 2748
Alexandria, VA 22301
(703) 836-5480

PRINTED IN THE UNITED STATES OF AMERICA

ISBN: 0-945981-58-9

Section One

Chapter 1

Taking Your Sport to College

It's the last race of the last meet of your senior year in high school. Time to put away your running shoes and all your sports memories and get on with life? No way!

College life and college sports are intertwined. And that doesn't mean just for the star football or basketball player for whom college may be a step on the road to a professional sports career.

College sports is a wide, wide world, encompassing everything from "factories" with facilities that make the pros jealous to intramurals at a small college where the only requirement is the energy to get out on the field.

And that is what this book is all about. Helping you—the STUDENT-athlete (the emphasis is intentional)—sort through all the confusion and make a correct decision about where and how you will take your sport (or sports) to college.

This book is not aimed at the blue-chipper whose postal carrier has been groaning under the weight of mail from college coaches and whose phone has been ringing off the hook. He or she, however, might do well to read the chapter on rules and how to avoid the violations that keep bursting into the headlines.

Our goal is to make the path a bit smoother for the better- than-average high school athlete who wants to keep competing while pursuing his or her college degree. To that end, we will tell you how scholarships and partial scholarships are awarded; how to match your athletic and academic skills with the right college; and how to use your sports to give you a winning edge in admission to those tough-to-get-into small colleges with strong sports traditions.

Along the way, we will explore the roles of other important players—your parents, your high school coaches, your guidance counselors. We will tell you how to attract the notice of college coaches and how best to follow through once you have their interest.

To make your search for a college scholarship a little easier, we have included charts with the addresses and athletic department phone numbers for schools in the three divisions of the National Collegiate Athletic Association and also the 480 mostly smaller colleges in the National Association of Intercollegiate Athletics. For NCAA Division I schools, we also have included graduation rate information most of the schools provided to The Chronicle of Higher Education.

Mixed in with this you will find words of advice from some of America's most successful college coaches—from Penn State's Joe Paterno, whose football team is perennially one of the nation's best; to Sharon Goldbrenner of Trenton State, whose teams have won three Division III field hockey championships and three women's lacrosse crowns; to Jim Steen, the swimming coach at Kenyon College, whose men's teams have won 12 consecutive Division III championships and whose women's teams have won eight in a row.

Let's go back to the subject of graduation rates. In many ways, the issue epitomizes a period in which there have been nearly as many headlines about the problems and scandals of college sports as about what the teams did on the playing field. True, there are more than enough scandals to go around, but they do not typify the bulk of college sports.

The Chronicle of Higher Education found, for example, that a larger percentage of athletes at NCAA Division I schools (262 out of 295 responded to the survey) graduated within five years than did among the student bodies as a whole. For all students, 47.9 percent of those who entered in the fall of 1984 graduated by August 1989. But among athletes, 56.1 percent graduated in that same five-year period.

A closer look at the survey pinpoints how much big-time basketball and football have contributed to the image of a system that "uses" athletes, then casts them out without an education. Just 38.9 percent of recruited basketball players graduated in five years (some schools reported a 0.0 rate) and only 47.4 percent of football players. The figures are even worse among the schools that play major Division I-A football schedules. There, only 42.5 percent of football recruits got their diplomas in five years and just 31.9 percent of basketball players.

But there's another side of the picture for female athletes. Their graduation rate of 65.6 percent is far above both the figures for male athletes (52.7 percent) and that for students overall (47.9 percent).

The negative image that has plagued college sports in recent years goes beyond graduation rates, however. The Knight Foundation Commission on Intercollegiate Athletics came up with a wide-ranging list of recommendations to increase academic performance, impose tighter financial rules (including the outside income of coaches) and put the major responsibility for cleaning up sports on college presidents and trustees.

The message obviously is being heard. The NCAA convention in January 1991 saw college and university presidents assuming a tougher role. There were cuts in the number of coaches, in the number of scholarships (including football and basketball), and new restrictions on practice time, length of seasons and use of athletic dormitories. And these changes come on top of the more stringent entrance and eligibility (Proposition 48) rules adopted in recent years.

Problems still remain. Many major football and basketball schools still enroll athletes with academic records and test scores well below what it takes for non-athletes to win admission. This has led one of the regional accrediting groups, the Southern Association of Colleges and Schools, to consider linking academic accreditation to the integrity of a school's sports programs. This would add a powerful new weapon for cleaning up college sports. While the NCAA can only impose sanctions on a college's sports programs, loss of accreditation could have crippling consequences for a school—including a cutoff of federal financial aid to its students.

For all the evidence that the NCAA has turned the corner, the road back to sports respectability undoubtedly still has many bumps ahead.

"There's no doubt we are moving in the right direction," says Charles Cavagnaro, who was named athletic director at Memphis State University in the wake of a scandal over the low graduation rate of its basketball players, "but we still have a way to go. For one thing, schools have to end this 'arms race' we're in. You know, I build a weight room and you have to build a bigger, fancier one."

All the headlines, it becomes apparent, really don't have much to do with the average college student-athlete for whom this book is intended. Just consider that 266,368 students—89,212 women and 177,156 men—participated in intercollegiate athletics at NCAA schools in 1989-90 and compare that to the number of sports scandals. There is ample room for you—the typical STUDENT-athlete—to make college sports an important and pleasurable part of higher education.

And now back to that final race—and we sincerely hope you will have started thinking about your athletic future long before the end of your senior year. This is a complicated process with many options for both student and college. To compete successfully, you need an early start and plenty of support. That's what this book aims to provide.

Chapter 2

The Wide, Wide World of Financial Aid

Financial aid and college athletics are like teammates. Quite simply, you may be able to use your athletic abilities to help pay the cost of your college education.

Note that we said "help pay." The "four-year free ride" is pretty well gone. It's still out there, mainly in football and basketball, but unless the coaches are already camping on your doorstep, don't count on it.

Your realistic goal, as a good to excellent athlete, should be to see how much of an athletic scholarship may be available—or to what extent your sports abilities may help you get into a school where you can qualify for financial assistance based on your individual needs.

CLASSIFYING THE COLLEGES

First let's take a look at how colleges and universities are classified. This governs the aid they can give their student-athletes.

NCAA Division I

These members of the National Collegiate Athletic Association are the "biggies," especially those with Division I-A—a further breakdown of this division—football programs. Into this group fall the major state universities and the independent sports powers you see on television. Guidelines specify that schools should compete "at the highest feasible level" in either football or basketball with the program being regional or national in scope.

Division I schools must offer at least six varsity sports for men's or mixed teams and six for women's teams. This will increase to seven sports in each category for the 1994-95 school year. Indoor and outdoor track may be counted as two sports.

Schools that have Division I-A football teams already must field teams in seven sports for men or mixed teams and seven for women. They also must have stadiums that seat at least 30,000, average 17,000 paid attendance at home games and play more than 60 percent of their football games against other Division I-A teams. In most cases, these are the teams you see in the big year-end bowl games competing for the "national championship." There is no Division I-A playoff, and the "champion" is selected by the Associated Press and United Press International polls.

Schools with Division I-AA football programs must play 60 percent of their football games against Division I-A or I-AA teams. There is a playoff for a national championship in Division I-AA.

All Division I schools are treated the same in every sport except football. In basketball, for example, both men's and women's teams may not play more than four games a year against opponents who are not in Division I. A minimum number of games or matches is specified for each sport.

Although these are the biggest sports operations, the NCAA has strict limits on how many scholarships may be awarded. And there are a few Division I schools, notably the Ivy League, that offer only need-based financial aid. As a general rule, Division I schools have very competitive programs and actively recruit athletes. Recent rules changes (increasing the number of varsity sports and requiring at least $250,000 in financial aid for both men's and women's sports, exclusive of football and basketball) have been aimed at those schools that were in Division I mainly for basketball—playing football at the Division II or III level. Effective in the 1993-94 school year, this will be barred. The schools will have to play football as part of a new Division I-AAA classification.

NCAA Division II

This division is just a step behind Division I in size of programs—it includes many smaller state-supported schools—but can be nearly as competitive in terms of seeking out athletes. The number of scholarships permitted is sharply lower than the Division I limit in football, but only slightly behind in most other sports.

Division II schools must offer four varsity sports for men or mixed teams and four for women. More than half of football and basketball games must be against Division I or Division II schools. The minimum number of contests required is lower than for Division I. There are national playoffs in football as well as in other sports.

NCAA Division III

No athletic scholarships are permitted. Financial aid is awarded solely on the basis of financial need. Student-athletes cannot be treated more favorably than other students. This group includes most of the prestigious small colleges with highly competitive admissions. Many of these have proud athletic rivalries and traditions, however, and your sports abilities can help you get in the door.

Division III schools must sponsor four varsity sports for men or mixed teams and four for women. The minimum number of contests is lower still than Division II. More than half of football and basketball games must be against other Division III colleges.

NAIA

Any four-year college is eligible for membership in the National Association of Intercollegiate Athletics, but its more than 480 schools tend to be smaller ones. The NAIA is organized by districts. There are post-season district tournaments in some sports as well as national championships. Many NAIA schools have excellent sports programs, and most offer some athletic scholarships. About 60 schools belong to both the NAIA and some division of the NCAA.

Other Classifications

Other organizations include the National Christian College Athletic Association (NCCAA), the National Bible College Athletic Association (NBCAA) and the National Little College Athletic Association (NLCAA). Member schools are often small church-affiliated colleges. They may or may not offer athletic scholarships. Many also belong to either the NAIA or the NCAA.

Exceptions to the Rule

How do you know which schools belong to what national organization and division? The tables in this book will help you. But remember, there are a few exceptions that may be important in helping you assess a college's sports program. A school is allowed to compete in a higher division in one men's and one women's sport (an exception, beginning in the 1991-92 school year, is women's basketball. Division II and III schools will no longer be permitted to play Division I schedules in that sport). In general, this happens when a school has a very competitive program in that sport, such as Division III Johns Hopkins' men's lacrosse team. On the other side of the coin, a school can play a lower division schedule in one sport (except football after 1993 as noted above), if it meets all the requirements (no athletic scholarships in a Division III sport, for example).

7

GRANTS-IN-AID: HOW MUCH?

Athletic scholarships, or grants-in-aid as the colleges call them, are generally limited by both the NCAA and the NAIA to tuition and fees, room and board and the cost of required course-related books. The exception is NCAA Division III schools where need alone, not athletic ability, determines the amount of financial help.

The NCAA also allows colleges to provide some need-based assistance above the grants-in-aid, but not to exceed $1400 a year in Division I ($900 a year in Division II). The total, however, can never exceed the average cost of attendance for that school. Each college has determined a figure for its average cost, and you need to find out what that is. It can have a major impact on the total aid package. If the average cost is just $1000 above the value of the grant-in-aid, for example, $1000 is the most an athlete could receive in need-based aid. If it is, say, $1500 above the grant total, then the extra aid could total the full $1400 allowed by the NCAA.

In figuring the total aid package, your family's ability to contribute is a factor. Pell Grant assistance from the federal government and work-study programs also count as part of the total. Student loans do not.

For Division III schools, all financial aid must be based on need and provided without consideration for athletic participation. It can include tuition, fees, room and board, books, transportation and incidental costs of attendance—again not to exceed the school's average attendance cost and not more than $900 above the grant-in-aid figure.

Need-based aid doesn't sound as glamorous as an athletic scholarship, but many Division III coaches point out that the total assistance over a four-year period may well be greater than you would get with a partial scholarship somewhere else. The test is how much it will cost you and your parents for you to graduate from college.

A note here about women's sports. Title IX of the Education Act of 1972 gave women a major boost. Title IX requires an equitable balance between the aid for men and women. Men still get more athletic scholarships, but the large rosters for football skew that statistic. In most other sports, the number of scholarships for women student-athletes is equal to—and in many cases greater than—the number open to men.

That does not means things are yet equal. The ratio of male to female college student-athletes remains almost 2-1. In 1989-90, men made up 66.51 percent of those participating in college sports, women 33.49 percent.

Judith M. Sweet, elected in 1991 as the first woman president of the NCAA, will continue to support the enforcement of Title IX. The Women's Sports Foundation, a nonprofit educational organization begun in 1974 by tennis great Billie Jean King, provides information services, publishes a list of women's intercollegiate athletic scholarships and actively advocates equal opportunities for women in sports (for details, call 1-800-227-398).

GRANTS-IN-AID: HOW MANY?

The numbers and types of athletic scholarships available vary widely with the school's classification and the sport. The formulas can get complicated, with an actual head count imposed in a few sports. In others, the limit is an equivalent of full scholarships, opening the way for coaches to split up their scholarship dollars among many more athletes. Here, in simplified form, are the limits:

NCAA Division I

In football, Division I-A institutions can have a total of 95 football players on scholarship at any one time, with that number dropping to 92 for the 1992-93 school year, to 88 for 1993-94 and to 85 for 1994-95. Division I-AA schools will cut their present limit of 70 full grants-in-aid in football by 10 percent over the same three-year period.

Division I basketball programs, both women's and men's, will have the present limit of 15 scholarships cut to 14 for the 1992-93 school year and to 13 for 1993-94.

Both Division I-A football and Division I basketball have full scholarships only, with no splitting of grants permitted.

Other Division I sports with a limit on the total number of athletes on scholarship are: women's gymnastics, 10; women's tennis, 8; women's volleyball, 12. These numbers will be reduced by 10 percent beginning in 1992-93.

Men's sports with a limit based on an equivalent number of scholarships are: baseball, 13; cross country/track, 14; fencing, 5; golf, 5; gymnastics, 7; ice hockey, 20; lacrosse, 14; rifle, 4; skiing, 7; soccer, 11; swimming, 11; tennis, 5; volleyball, 5; water polo, 5; and wrestling, 11. These, too, will be reduced 10 percent in 1992-93.

Women's sports and their equivalency levels are: cross country/track, 16; fencing, 5; field hockey, 11; golf, 6; lacrosse, 11; skiing, 7; softball, 11; and swimming, 14. These also will be cut 10 percent beginning in 1992-93.

NCAA Division II

All sports are subject to an equivalency test rather than a head count. Football squads, for example, are limited to the equivalent of 40 scholarships in any academic year, with this number being cut by 10 percent in 1992-93.

Other present scholarship maximums (to be cut 10 percent effective with the start of the 1992-93 school year):

Men's sports: baseball, 10; basketball, 12; cross country/track, 14; fencing, 5; golf, 4; gymnastics, 6; ice hockey, 15; lacrosse, 12; rifle, 4; skiing, 7; soccer, 10; swimming, 9; tennis, 5; volleyball, 5; water polo, 5; wrestling, 10.

There is an additional limitation for men in Division II. No school can provide more than 60 scholarships (or the equivalent) in sports other than football and basketball in any academic year.

Women's sports: basketball, 12; cross country/track, 14; fencing, 5; field hockey, 7; golf, 6; gymnastics, 6; lacrosse, 11; skiing, 7; soccer, 11; swimming, 9; tennis, 6; volleyball, 8.

NCAA Division III

Since aid is unrelated to athletics, there is no limit on how many student-athletes can be receiving need-based financial assistance.

NAIA

There currently is no limit on the number of scholarships that can be awarded in any sport. But many small schools have limited budgets, and the number of scholarships is limited by the cash available.

PARTIAL SCHOLARSHIPS

A close look at the limits on sports scholarships—other than those in football and basketball, which are the "revenue sports" that keep college athletic programs solvent—makes it easy to understand why partial scholarships have become such a major part of the picture.

A swimming coach in Division I could not begin to fill all the lanes in a meet if he gave his 11 scholarships to 11 male athletes (or 14 females). And it's even harder in Division II with a limit of 9 apiece for men and women. But if the coach fragments those scholarships—room and board to a diver, tuition for a freestyler, books to a backstroker—he can put more bodies into the pool and field a more competitive team.

When Wichita State won the College World Series in 1989, not one member of the

9

team was on a full scholarship. Coach Gene Stephenson had split his 13 full grants-in-aid 27 different ways. Although he says he thinks all of his players deserved a full scholarship, he was doing the most he could with the resources at hand.

This scenario is repeated season after season in most of the "non-revenue" sports— those that take in less at the gate than it takes to field a team. Prospective students must work out the best arrangements they can.

It should be noted that the number of scholarships listed are the limit; a college may well not fund all the scholarships available in some of the minor sports. For this reason, many athletic directors say the 10 percent cut will not hurt the minor sports—and could even be a help in some cases. Their reasoning: many of the scholarships being "cut" are not funded anyway. The football and basketball grants being cut, however, are funded in almost all cases and that may make some money available for minor sports.

Although NAIA coaches face no limits in numbers, partial scholarships are often used to help stretch the budget to cover more student-athletes.

OUT-OF-STATE TUITION WAIVERS

Another way for colleges, especially state-supported ones, to provide aid is to waive the extra tuition charged out-of-state students. This can amount to several thousand dollars, depending on the school. There also are ways to work out financial aid arrangements that couple a tuition waiver with a partial scholarship. Ask about this when conferring with any college or university.

HOW LONG, HOW LONG

When we mentioned earlier that the "four-year free ride" was a thing of the past, we were referring not only to the limits on how much aid, but also the length of the commitment.

Basic grants-in-aid can be for a period not to exceed five years, but the aid is provided just one year at a time. Prospective athletes can be told, under NCAA rules, that the athletic department will recommend renewal of the aid each year for four years—and even that such recommendations have always been followed in the past. The renewal is not automatic, however, and prospects have to be informed about this.

The same rules apply to continued aid to a student-athlete who is injured in competition. The athletic department can tell prospects about the school's usual policy in renewing aid to athletes who are injured or become ill. Again, renewal is not automatic for injured athletes, and prospects cannot be told it is.

An appeals process within the school is available to student-athletes whose financial aid is either reduced or canceled.

Need-based aid also is on a year-to-year basis. The student must remain in good academic standing. His or her family's finances must be reviewed to determine whether there has been a major change in the ability to contribute toward that student's education costs. In other words, if your parents hit the lottery or, conversely, the family farm goes under, the school wants to know!

These are all points to ask about when you get around to talking to colleges or universities you may attend.

A WORLD OF DIFFERENCES

Not all colleges are created equal: even the big-name sports schools vary widely in the levels of financial aid they offer their athletes. The major state universities, for example, can usually be counted on to provide close to the maximum amount of aid permitted by

NCAA rules. But the Ivy League—Yale, Harvard, Princeton, Pennsylvania, etc.—offers only need-based aid even though it plays a Division I schedule.

Even a Division I basketball powerhouse such as Georgetown University plays a Division III schedule in football (this will have to change for the 1993-94 school year) and offers no athletic scholarships in several of its minor sports. On the other hand, Johns Hopkins University in Baltimore is a Division III school—except in lacrosse where it plays a Division I schedule, awards scholarships and annually challenges for the national title.

In checking out a college or university, you need to find out exactly how many scholarships are available in your sport and how they are likely to be split up.

Chapter 3
The Rules of the Game

The official National Collegiate Athletic Association policy manual, updated yearly, is about the size of a telephone book. Its 399 pages might well have been written by a team of corporate lawyers. The rules are extremely complicated and can be confusing. But they are the rules—and they apply to you just as surely as they do to the 40-point-a-game scorer being courted by every Division I school in the country.

It is your responsibility to learn what the rules are and to operate within them. The consequences of breaking them can be disastrous both to the student-athlete and the college or university. The student can be declared ineligible. The school can be barred from post-season play and/or television appearances, be put on probation, lose scholarships, even—in the most flagrant cases—the "death sentence" of being barred from intercollegiate competition for a season or more.

Enforcement of the rules is getting stricter every year. You've seen the stories in the newspaper and on television: big name schools called on the carpet for everything from charges of sending cash to a player's parents to driving an ineligible player to class. Pro sports agents have been tried for signing and paying players while they still played college sports.

To help you stay away from trouble, the NCAA publishes each year a handy "Guide for the College-Bound Student-Athlete." It is sold in bulk (50 copies for $12.00 from the NCAA, 6201 College Blvd., Overland Park, KS, 66211-2422). Your guidance department should have one. Get a copy. It's a good reference for you and your parents. The National Association of Intercollegiate Athletics has a similar "Guide for the College Bound Student." It is also available in bulk (50 copies for $15.00); single copies are free from NAIA, 1221 Baltimore, Kansas City, Mo. 64105.

Here are some of the basic rules to help keep you on the right side of the NCAA.

WHEN IS A PROFESSIONAL NOT A PROFESSIONAL?

The attitude of colleges toward professional sports has changed markedly in recent years, but there are still some strict conditions.

You CANNOT be eligible for intercollegiate athletics in any sport if you have:

- Agreed to be represented generally, rather than in a specific sport, by an agent or organization that will market your athletic ability or reputation.
- After becoming a college student-athlete, accept pay for or allow your name and picture to be used for advertising or promoting the sale of any commercial product or service.

You CANNOT be eligible in your particular sport if you have:

- Signed a professional contract, asked that your name be put on a pro draft list, actually played on a professional team, taken pay or accepted the promise of pay in any form.
- Agreed to be represented by an agent or other marketing organization.
- Tried out with a professional sport organization while enrolled in college.

You CAN be eligible for competition in a sport other than the one for which you have been paid (you played minor league baseball, you can still play college basketball). You also still can be eligible if:

- Prior to enrolling in college you tried out for a professional sport, even if you received expenses for the tryout, or if, before enrolling, you were paid to give instruction in a particular sport.
- You received compensation authorized by the U.S. Olympic Committee for loss of employment while preparing for or participating in the Olympic Games.

A student-athlete who is under contract to or receiving pay from a professional team cannot receive financial aid. But he or she can become eligible for aid again by severing ties with the pro sport, even if still bound by an option clause in a contract. Starting professional competition again while still having college eligibility left, however, is considered a violation of ethical conduct rules and means a ban from all intercollegiate sports.

DANGLING PROPOSITIONS

Academic requirements for student-athletes have been toughened in recent years. Much of the furor over something called Proposition 48, and the further tightening under Proposition 42 in January 1989, has faded. But the rules, now referred to by the NCAA as Bylaw 14.3, are still very much in effect. A bit of history may be in order.

Proposition 48

This rule went into effect for the 1986-87 school year amid rising concern that schools were admitting athletes who were unable to meet college-level academic demands. In addition to the basic requirement that incoming student-athletes have a high school diploma and an overall 2.0 (C) grade point average, the NCAA said that to be eligible in Division I and II schools they also must:

1. Have a C (2.0) average in a "core curriculum" of 11 basic academic courses. These must include three units of English, two of mathematics, two of social science, two (including one laboratory course) units of natural or physical science and two other courses that can be from the above areas or can include foreign language, computer science, philosophy or nondoctrinal religion.
2. Score a minimum 700 (out of 1,600) on the Scholastic Aptitude Test (SAT) or 18 (out of 36) on the American College Test (ACT). (The standards are almost certain to get tougher in the future, with the next NCAA convention expected to endorse a rule requiring a 2.5 average in 13 core courses. The new rules would go into effect in 1995.)

Student-athletes who met one, but not both, of the new standards were designated as "partial qualifiers." They could still be admitted to the college and receive athletic scholarships, but could not play or practice in their sport during their freshman year while they proved they could handle college-level academics. Eligibility for partial qualifiers became three years in Divisions I and II, compared to four for other student-athletes.

Proposition 42

The NCAA tightened the rules another notch at its January 1989 convention by deciding that, beginning in the 1990-91 school year, partial qualifiers no longer could receive athletic scholarships in their freshman year. That led to Georgetown basketball coach John Thompson's highly publicized boycott of two games and similar—if less dramatic—protests from many other coaches. They claimed the SAT and ACT were biased

13

against minorities, and the loss of student aid would keep many black athletes out of colleges.

Proposition 48, as tightened by Proposition 42, remains in effect. It has been modified only slightly, to allow partial qualifiers to receive need-based financial aid from the school during their freshman year.

Whether you call it Bylaw 14.3 or Proposition 48, these NCAA rules address only the absolute minimum academic levels that can be accepted. For an athlete to be recruited at that level of academic skill, he or she must have extraordinary athletic skills. The average student-athlete must do much better in the classroom to have a chance of going on to collegiate play. In the choosy colleges, athletic skills may be a big help in running the admissions hurdles, but only if your grades and test scores put you on the playing field for that school.

These rules do not presently apply to Division III colleges. Eligibility for financial aid, practice and competition in Division III are governed by institutional, conference and other NCAA rules.

NAIA Rules

NAIA rules are less complex. To be eligible for sports in your freshman year, you must meet two out of three criteria: Graduate in the top half of your high school class; have an overall 2.0 GPA; score 700 on the SAT or 18 on the ACT. Those who don't qualify must sit out of sports for a year.

There are also NAIA benchmarks for continued competition. A student-athlete must have 24 semester hours of credit to play a second season, 48 for a third season and 72 (including 48 in general education or her or his major) for a fourth. Students must also maintain a 2.0 GPA to compete in their third and fourth years or have junior class standing or higher.

We'll go into the challenge of matching your academic skills with the right college in a later chapter.

THE RECRUITER WANTS YOU

The recruiting of college student-athletes is a highly complicated—and tightly regulated—operation. As an average- to-good athlete, your challenge is probably going to be to catch the eye of a college coach or recruiter, not fend them off. Still, you need to know the rules so you can avoid any costly misstep in this sensitive area.

NCAA Recruiting Rules—The Highlights

- You become a "prospective student-athlete" when you enter the ninth grade—earlier if a college or university provides you (or your relatives or friends) any financial aid or other benefits that it does not provide to prospective students generally.

- You become a "recruited prospective student-athlete" at a college if a coach or other "representative" of the college's athletic interests (booster or representative) solicits you or any member of your family for the purpose of securing your enrollment and participation in intercollegiate athletics at that college.

- Actions that make you a recruited prospective student-athlete include providing you transportation to the campus, entertaining you or any member of your family in any way on the campus (an exception is a free ticket to an athletic event when you visit with a group, such as your high school team), placing telephone calls to you or any member of your family, or visiting you or any member of your family anywhere other than the college campus.

- A "representative of an institution's athletic interests" is anyone the college has asked to help recruit a student or anyone the school knows is trying to recruit for them. This includes boosters, alumni and such. Representatives are governed by the same rules as staff members, and schools are responsible for their actions. They are barred from recruiting in Division I, and their activities are limited in Division II. This limitation does not apply to alumni or representatives if the contact is part of the college's regular admissions program for all prospective students, including nonathletes.

- Under a recent rules change, a college coach can contact you in person off the college campus only on or after July 1 following your junior year in high school. Phone calls from coaches or faculty members also are barred before July 1 following your junior year, and coaches may not accept collect calls from you before that date. Division III coaches, alumni and boosters can contact you any time after you complete your junior year.

- You can make one 48-hour expense-paid trip to a college, but not before classes have started in your senior year. The school can pay for transportation (tourist class only if flying), room and board (at on-campus facilities if available) and modest entertainment. (A college host can be given $20 a day to cover all costs of entertaining you. But beware, this can't go for T-shirts or other such mementos. T-shirts, sweatshirts and caps have gotten more than one college in trouble.) The school also can entertain parents or legal guardians during that one trip.

  Effective Aug. 1, 1992, the college may not provide the trip unless you have furnished the school a score from an SAT, ACT or PSAT taken on a national test date under national testing conditions.

- In all, you can make expense-paid visits to a total of five NCAA Division I and Division II schools. This applies even if you are being recruited in more than one sport.

- You can visit a campus as many times as you want at your own expense. You do not have to wait to make these trips until your senior year. During those visits, a Division I school can provide up to three complimentary tickets to a campus athletic event—but nothing else. Division II schools can also provide a meal at an on-campus facility.

- Just three in-person recruiting contacts with a prospect or his or her family at any location off the campus are permitted in Divisions I and II. In Divisions I and II the contact must be made by an athletic department staff member who has been authorized to recruit. No funds may be spent for entertaining the student or her or his family. Coaches may evaluate you by watching practices or games on four occasions. A tournament that is held on consecutive days counts as one evaluation. There is no limit on contacts in Division III.

- A college staffer or representative can describe the school's grant-in-aid program and recommend a prospect for receiving such aid—but must make it clear that only the school's regular financial aid authority can actually award aid. Only after that authority provides written notice of the amount, duration and kinds of aid is it official.

- A school may ask a prospect to undergo a medical examination by the regular team physician during his or her official on-campus visit. But Division I or Division III schools may not conduct, either on campus or off, any kind of practice or workout in which the student demonstrates his athletic ability.

- Division II schools can, with permission of your high school athletic director, hold a tryout before enrollment but after you have completed your high school eligibility. This may include tests to evaluate your strength, speed, agility and sports skills. It may include competition in some sports, but not in football, ice hockey, lacrosse, soccer or wrestling.

  NAIA schools can hold on-campus tryouts if that is a general practice—such as having auditions for music majors.

Developmental clinics that are open to the general public and are designed to develop fundamental skills are not considered tryouts.

- There are strict limits on what the college can provide a prospective student-athlete in terms of brochures or other printed information. And watch out for those T-shirts, caps and like items. They're a definite no-no.

DRUG POLICIES AND PROCEDURES

NCAA regulations require your consent for drug testing before participating in intercollegiate competition in any sports. Such testing occurs on a year-round basis. If you test positive for any banned substance, including steroids, you will be ineligible for further intercollegiate competition, subject to an appeal for restoration of your eligibility. Many schools and conferences also have their own policies on drug use.

OTHER PITFALLS

You may be contacted by a scouting service during high school. You should be aware that the NCAA does not sanction or endorse any such service and specifically prohibits them from receiving compensation based on the amount of the college scholarships you may be awarded. If you have a question about whether the scouting service meets NCAA rules, check it out with the NCAA office.

After your high school eligibility is over, football and basketball prospects can participate in only two high school all- star games in each sport. After starting your senior year in high school, you cannot participate in a sports camp or clinic held by an NCAA college.

The NCAA guide also reminds student-athletes that they must sign a statement each academic year about eligibility, recruitment, financial aid and amateur status. And it warns:

"Do not jeopardize your eligibility through involvement in violations of NCAA legislation. Knowingly furnishing the NCAA or your college false or misleading information about your involvement or knowledge of an NCAA rules violation will make you ineligible."

Chapter 4
Another Basic—Appraising Sports Skills

Now comes the difficult part for both parents and student-athletes. You know what colleges can offer in the way of athletic scholarships and other financial aid for student-athletes. You know enough about the rules of the NCAA and other organizations to avoid any pitfalls.

But how do you match up your individual sports skills to the proper level—indeed the proper school—for college play?

APPRAISING YOUR SKILLS

College coaches agree that one of the toughest tasks facing the college-bound student-athlete is a realistic appraisal of talent. How good are you? Can you play on a Division I or II team? Would you really be better off at a Division III school or some other small college?

Obviously, you need a hand in this. Your high school coach is a key player. More than anyone else, she or he can point you in the right direction. Of course there is more to choosing a college than checking only the athletic program. Your guidance counselor will help you with meeting the academic requirements of the college. Your parents will have to be involved in decisions regarding cost, distance from home, etc.

Those relationships will be examined in other chapters, but for right now there is no escaping the bottom line. This is your life and your decision, and you must be the one to face reality. The appraisal process is more difficult for some student-athletes than for others.

If college coaches and recruiters have been calling already, then someone else has made that appraisal for you. College sports professionals have decided your skills seem to match their level of competition. But high school students trying to catch the eye of a college coach don't have that free ride.

A side note here about recruiting: it comes in all shapes and forms. If you are a superstar, the sky's the limit as far as interest is concerned. For other student-athletes, a more common situation involves receiving questionnaires from colleges that have heard about them. How does the word get out? The sports pages, contact with high school coaches, letters or calls from alumni, etc.

This questionnaire will inquire whether you have any interest in the school and ask you to answer a number of questions about your athletic and academic accomplishments. By all means, take advantage of these. Answer promptly and completely, working with your parents, coach and guidance counselor to do the best job you can. Questionnaires provide chances for you to introduce yourself to colleges. But be aware, a college may send out hundreds of these forms, and the interest may go no farther.

You probably won't be hearing from a college in this fashion before early in your senior season (a new rule bars any phone call or off-campus contact by a Division I or Division II coach until July 1 after the end of your junior year). By then you should be well on the way to an assessment of your athletic prospects.

A skill appraisal always is easier for a student from a large school in a populous area. If you are such a student, you will likely have been exposed to a highly competitive sports scene. You will have played with or against athletes who have gone on to college sports. Are you as good as they were? Better?

You also can check to find out how they did on the college level. Did they pick a school where they were able to compete and make sports an enjoyable part of their college lives? Or did they select the wrong place and end up sitting on the bench or, worse, dropping out?

The mistakes of others can be a great guide.

A student-athlete in a small town or rural area may not have the same advantage. High school competition can be spotty with few college-level athletes to compare skills.

Realistic skill appraisals are much easier in some sports than in others. A track and field athlete's times and distances, a golfer's scores, a swimmer's times, a skier's point profile, a rower's ergometer test statistics; all are hard facts that can be presented to a college coach.

But other athletic skills are more subjective. A football player can have great 40-yard speed but not be able to elude tacklers after fielding a punt, or carry a ball without fumbling. A basketball player may have a great vertical leap measurement, but can she rebound in heavy traffic?

SPORTS CAMPS

Sports camps, summer leagues, AAU swim teams and other such activities are great places to attract some attention. You need to be selective, however, especially where sports camps are concerned.

If you have your eye on a particular school which conducts a camp in your sport, by all means sign up. One of the stars of Indiana University's championship soccer team first came to the coach's attention at camp when he was just 12 years old. But you must use good judgment.

Don't enroll in a famous coach's camp if your own good sense tells you his or her college is way out of your league. Also, beware of some camps that advertise a huge roster of professional stars. Check to see whether these celebrities actually work with campers or just drop by to sign a few autographs.

Many coaches will not pay much attention to you at a camp until the summer after your sophomore year. You simply won't have matured enough. The summer after your junior year is when the serious looking is done. Keep that in mind if you are thinking about a camp that is far from home or very expensive.

TOURNAMENTS

District, regional and state tournaments in sports such as golf or tennis offer a real opportunity to be noticed. Good scores or high finishes in such competition are something a college coach can appreciate. A 76 in a tournament may tell a golf coach more about your potential than a 72 practice round on your home course with no pressure. If your goal is to attend a school in your home state, concentrate your tournament efforts there. But if your aim is broader, you may have to shoot for a regional or larger stage on which to show what you can do.

NEVER, NEVER USE STEROIDS

Don't let the desire to play college sports lead you to do something stupid and dangerous. A frightening number of high school athletes have experimented with anabolic (the word means "tissue-building") steroids and other performance-enhancing drugs. The quick gains in size and strength are enticing, but the long-term medical consequences should shock anyone out of the notion. Physically, steroids can cause heart problems and liver and kidney damage, possibly cancer. Mentally, steroid use results in increased anger and aggressiveness and often includes nightmares, hallucinations and depression, sometimes suicide.

Tragic stories are becoming all too common, as the health consequences of using steroids begin to kick in. Listen to Lyle Alzado, pro football superstar and victim of an inoperable brain cancer he blamed on steroid use which for years he denied. He told *Sports Illustrated*, "I lied. I'm sorry success meant so much to me. If you're on steroids or human growth hormone, stop. I should have."

Testing programs are becoming more prevalent, as the need for reform gains more support among sports authorities and athletes themselves, but concern for your own body, not a fear of being caught, should be the major consideration.

Also, any college coach who would condone use of such substances is not someone you want to be around.

PRESENTING YOUR SKILLS

It is up to you, the student-athlete, to prepare a realistic analysis of your skills and put it in a format that will catch a college coach's eye. This should include all the physical facts about you—height, weight, speed, etc.—as well as a summary of your personal and team accomplishments. Don't pad this with things you can't back up, but don't leave any pertinent facts out either. Try to give the coach an accurate feel for what you have accomplished in sports and what you hope to do at the college level.

A good way to do this is to prepare a sports resume, following the guidelines adults use in applying for jobs. Detailed information about preparing a sports resume is included in Chapter 7 and Appendix A of this book.

If your real value to the team is not the points you score but the help—both on and off the field—you give teammates, college coaches need to know that. Coaches realize they can't have a star in every slot, and besides, they need players with the kind of spirit that makes a team a good working unit.

If you have a sportsmanship award as evidence of your team spirit, list it on your resume. If not, don't hesitate to mention this quality in the cover letter that goes with your resume.

The helping hand of your high school coach is a vital ingredient. We will talk more about that in Chapter 7.

Chapter 5
Parents and the Process

"Be responsible for who you are and what you do" is the advice to student-athletes from a staff member of the University of South Carolina Athletic Department.

You should keep this thought in your mind during the important process of finding the right place for your college education. Obviously the USC staffer has seen enough of student-athletes and their parents to feel her recommendation for responsibility was top priority when asked for her opinion.

THE IDEAL SITUATION FOR A CLOSE-TO-PERFECT PROCESS

First, your parents (and surely they are not skipping this chapter) realize the goal is a college where you will get the finest academic education you can handle, plus make lifelong friendships and compile happy memories of the playing fields. If financial aid from sports can help achieve that goal, so much the better.

Second, you accept the responsibility for giving it your best. In the words of St. Jerome, "No athlete is crowned save by the sweat of his own brow."

But the venerated saint probably didn't have a mother and father who had given up many hours driving him to practices since the day he first stepped up to the plate in a T-ball league.

You in turn recognize and appreciate the hopes and dreams your parents have for you. They cheered you on when you won and cheered you up when you lost, and they don't intend to stop now. Try to understand this, work together and remember this is the close-to-perfect situation. Many students reading this know the other side—listening to the excuses of parents who were just "too busy to get to the game," time after time after time.

In the ideal situation, you and your parents start the serious planning in your sophomore year. No big pressure, just becoming acquainted with admission rules, reading up on colleges, getting to know your high school coaches, teachers and your guidance counselors. Because you and your parents take the time to do this, college visits can be planned with no last-minute rush, you take all the right courses and pre-college academic tests, and you get an accurate assessment of your athletic level of play.

If you are a blue-chipper, your parents make it their business to learn all the high-pressure recruiting techniques so they won't be carried away by guarantees of glory.

Now you are ready to apply to colleges. With the help of your high school coaches and guidance counselors, you have a realistic idea of whether and where you can get some kind of financial aid based on your athletic talent. Or you know where you can continue playing your sport as an enrichment of your college experience.

You send in applications on time (don't forget to make copies) and wait for acceptances. When they arrive, you and your parents consider all the options. You make the final decision, your parents tell you how proud they are, and everybody celebrates at your favorite restaurant.

MORE REALISTIC SITUATION

That was the ideal. What's the reality?

Divorce isn't fatal, but statistics show that many of you won't be making these decisions with Mom and Dad sitting around the dining room table drinking hot chocolate.

That's OK, too. Depending on your special situation, your parents can still go through all the research and give you the support you need. It's important to know that if relationships are not friendly, your coach and guidance counselor or a caring teacher, while not getting in the middle of family problems, can provide help, information, a calm voice and support.

Here's another possible scenario. What about the Football Father who has made it very clear his major goal in life is seeing Sonny follow in his footsteps at old State U? Fine, if that's what Sonny wants, too, and if he can make it through the admission process. That may not be as easy as it was 25 years ago, and Dad needs to know that.

The opposite of this situation is the father or mother who was an unsuccessful athlete but wants to enjoy the thrill of victory through talented children. This can be a delightful family experience, of course, when treated with joy and pride. But not with pressure.

Problems also arise when parents have unrealistic estimates of their children's talents. This can happen in large city high schools, but it's more likely to occur in a small town where an average young athlete becomes a star because the competition is less fierce. College coaches spend a lot of time dealing with parents whose child has been rejected for a scholarship or admission and who keep saying, "But she was the star of every game in high school."

This should start you and your family thinking. Let's go back to how parents can help.

PREPARE YOUR STUDENT TO LEAVE HOME

More than one university athletic administrator named good old-fashioned homesickness as one of the biggest problems many families don't face up to when choosing a college. The family is so excited over a scholarship (or admission to a certain prized school) that everyone forgets the student will be far from home for the first time.

Long distance from home means no longer will the student-athlete hear the cheers of his family at every game, no small matter when this support may be at the heart of her athletic experience. At its worst, homesickness can cause a student-athlete to drop out—a real tragedy for the student and a significant one for the coach and team.

The point here is not whether growing up involves knowing how to be independent. Certainly, it does, but some students are simply not ready to do it. If they have a bad experience first time out in college, they may never make the break to mature adulthood.

Obviously, thousands of students make this transition with no trouble. One athletic director said some student-athletes can hardly wait to get away from well-meaning but domineering parents who second-guess their and the coaches' every move.

Take time to know where you honestly fit into this picture.

DEALING WITH STRESS

Suppose you get a sports scholarship of some kind. You and your parents need to realize that puts stress on you to produce results. Can you handle this?

Parents of a high school track star turned down a sports scholarship for their daughter because they did not want her to feel she ever had to put sports above academics. The pressure she might impose on herself concerned them, and this was part of a family discussion.

Her sports talents still helped her gain admission to the university, where she is a member of the track team.

Each family is different. Not all could afford to turn down scholarship help. The lesson here is that families need to understand each other. What one student can handle, another may not be able to manage.

UNDERSTAND FINANCIAL AID

There is one place in the process where family preparation is vital and can pay off. Much of the assistance for student-athletes we have been discussing includes at least some need-based aid. This is a vital part of your financial planning for college.

Quite simply, "need" is the difference between what it costs to attend a college and what your family can afford to contribute toward your education. The calculation sounds simple, but it depends on the college's financial aid office having all the figures it needs to work with. They know the top line—how much it costs to attend—but you and your family have to supply the bottom line.

That means starting early, because financial aid often is on a first-come, first-served basis. Get a good book on financial aid and learn the ins and outs of financial aid forms. Many factors enter into this equation—not only assets such as the value of your home but "liabilities" such as the number of brothers and sisters of college age. You should have backup materials, including copies of tax returns, readily at hand. For a detailed examination of the financial aid process, get *Don't Miss Out* ($7.50 postpaid) by Anna and Robert Leider (to order, write Octameron Associates, PO Box 2748, Alexandria, VA 22301).

You can still receive an athletic grant-in-aid or partial scholarship even if your family's contribution is substantial.

And remember that some of the Division III schools, where all aid is based on need, are very expensive. You may be eligible for assistance even if your family is prepared to be a lot of help.

File early! College after college echoed these words. Financial aid funds are limited, especially at some smaller schools, and it is often the case of the early applicant getting the financial dollar. It's up to your family to see that you are at the front of the line.

Nobody says this is going to be easy, but some honest discussion is bound to pay off for both you and your parents. They can help you find the best place for you and your sport. Then it's up to you to make the most of it.

Chapter 6
Guidance Counselors—Part of the Team

Your guidance counselor is another key player in your search for the winning edge.

Chances are your guidance counselor is trying to serve the needs of many students. Helping you with your college search is just one of his or her duties. Finding specialized scholarships adds another dimension to the equation of you, college and financial aid.

You must take the responsibility of letting your guidance counselor know what you are looking for. Your coach, counselor and parents are all there to help you, but you must not expect anyone else to carry the ball for you. Take the initiative early on in developing a relationship with your counselor. Ideally, one or both of your parents should be involved with the guidance office also.

COLLEGE RESOURCES

Your guidance counselor has information available to help you make choices. As the two of you work together through your high school career, your counselor will be the key resource for helping match your academic talents with the right colleges.

Some larger high schools have career and college centers with computer programs devoted to college information. If you don't have access to that kind of sophisticated software, your guidance counselor still should have books and manuals to start you on the way.

START EARLY

"Start early" is the advice given by absolutely everyone. Guidance counselors shake their heads in frustration when students rush in at the last minute. For anyone wanting sports scholarships, it's impossible.

When is early? Since many high schools assign counselors who remain with a student throughout his or her high school career, it's not too early to mention your goals in your freshman year. A sophomore year start may be about right for most students, but waiting until you are a junior to start the preliminary planning is pushing your luck.

Your goals may change from what they were in your sophomore year, of course, but if your guidance counselor gets to know you, he or she can begin to do exactly what the title implies—"guide" you through the process.

DON'T FORGET ACADEMICS

Don't forget a major function of the counselor—to help you choose courses that will provide the right foundation for your college career. That's the correct thing to do—and the NCAA rules demand it. You must have taken the right "core" academic courses to even be eligible for a scholarship. And you can't catch up on three years of neglect in your senior year.

Former Washington Redskin Dexter Manley's courageous confession that he couldn't read although he graduated from Oklahoma State University won't change such tragedies overnight, but more and more people are concerned.

U.S. Senator Bill Bradley of New Jersey and U.S. Representative Tom McMillen of

Maryland are pushing legislation to require public disclosure of graduation rates. That legislation is still pending.

For the first time, Division I-A and Division I universities (with a few exceptions) voluntarily furnished graduation statistics, which were published in the Chronicle of Higher Education. These are included in our charts for those NCAA divisions and discussed in Chapter 1. You should definitely ask the college admission and athletic staff people you talk to for this information.

Your counselor will be looking for a combination—a good academic "fit" for you plus the best place for you to use your sports talents, whether good enough for a scholarship or good enough to get you into a small prestigious school because of your athletic ability.

YOUR COUNSELOR DOESN'T WORK ALONE

Counselors have to consult with specialists regarding many of their students. A young violinist in the school orchestra may want to use her or his musical talent in the same way you want to use your athletic ability. The guidance counselor consults an expert—the music teacher—for information about the student's chances.

In your case, the counselor will work with your coach, first to get his or her evaluation of your talent, and then, ideally, to cooperate with the coach in getting you into the right college with as much financial aid as possible. We will go into specifics on the admission application process in a later chapter.

Encourage your parents to meet with guidance counselors. Counselors can relieve a lot of stress by providing answers to baffling questions such as, "How do we get an idea of what colleges are right for Susie?" They have the computer programs and books, they know the admission process, they know college admissions people, and helping students is their business.

Chapter 7
Help from the Coach

In the search for a college and an athletic scholarship or other financial aid, your high school coach is the person in the middle.

At every stage of your search, you will need to work with and rely on your coach. He or she often holds the key to your sports future. But how they use that key depends in large measure on you.

Coaches want to see their players do well in college. They really like young people or they wouldn't be coaching. Successful college athletes reflect credit on their high school coaches and their teaching abilities. But a coach can be a very busy person. You are going to be asking him or her to do even more. So it will be good for you to do some groundwork.

LAYING THE GROUNDWORK—YOUR SOPHOMORE YEAR

It should go without saying that developing a good relationship with your high school coach is most important if you hope to continue your athletic career. If you have been a disruptive, rebellious member of a team—in and out of the coach's doghouse—do you really expect that coach to go the extra mile to help you get into college or win some financial aid?

You should level with your coach about your ambitions as early as possible. There are always some athletic late-bloomers, but most future college athletes show signs of their abilities by their sophomore year. That's not too early to ask your coach the hard question: "Do you think I have the ability to play college sports?"

The coach's answer may well be a conditional one; for example, "Yes, but only if you improve certain facets of your game." This can be the basis of a frank and continuing dialogue. A coach does you no favor by building up your hopes and expectations beyond what your skills merit.

Along with your guidance counselor and your parents, the coach plays a key role in your initial narrowing down of possible colleges. Even at this early state, it's a complicated mix of considerations. The sports program should be within range of your athletic abilities, taking into account the improvement two more years of competition and physical maturity will bring. The academic program should be within reach of your scholastic abilities (what do your grades up to now show you can handle?). The size of the college and its distance from home should be within the scope that you and your parents think is best for you.

Many factors still can change. In your junior year, for example, your higher-than-expected PSAT score suggests more academic opportunities; your sudden growth spurt makes you a better athlete; your curve ball finds the strike zone instead of the dirt. Allowances can be made for changes, but it's hard to recover from a tardy start.

This is the time for an early dose of reality. Your sports skills may be good enough to get you onto the playing fields of Amherst, Williams or some other prestigious small college. But your grades aren't in the same league, and your parents are wary about your going to school a long way from home. On the other hand, your grades almost surely would get you into the University of Nebraska, but the sports scene there is way over your head.

The solution? Find some schools in the middle that fit your academic and sports profile. Remember, you are not locking in a final choice here, just selecting some terrain for further exploration.

25

PRELIMINARY INQUIRIES—YOUR SOPHOMORE YEAR

Your sophomore year is not too early to make preliminary inquiries about colleges that interest you. A brief letter to the coach indicating interest in his or her school and sport is appropriate. A little later you will be preparing more detailed communications, but some basic rules apply to both undertakings.

Be sure you have the right coach's name and that you spell it correctly. Nothing will help a letter find the wastebasket quicker than a wrong name. College coaches are a movable lot, so this book has not tried to list names. That might do you more harm than good. The charts in this book include telephone numbers for athletic departments in every institution in the NAIA and all divisions of the NCAA. Call before you write!

Your first letter also should demonstrate that you have some knowledge of that college's sports program. If it has won a conference championship or other honor, your letter should show that you are aware of that. You don't need to go into detail about your athletic skills at this stage. You are only a sophomore, remember, and have a lot of growing and learning to do. A mention that you will be looking for financial aid down the road is appropriate.

Don't expect great things from this first approach. At most you will probably get a sports brochure or media guide and a current schedule. But your name will go into a file, and who knows, a college recruiter checking out another athlete may cast an eye in your direction.

REFINING THE LIST—YOUR JUNIOR YEAR

You will need to refine your list of possible schools as you go along. Your junior year is the time to begin making some serious decisions. Your athletic skills will be more fully developed, so you and your coach may now be able to make a more realistic assessment of just how your game will stack up for college. Can you be a Division I athlete, Division II, Division III?

The same thing holds true on the academic side. You will have taken the PSAT, which gives you some idea of how you will do when you take the SAT for the first time in the spring. If you didn't do as well as expected, it may be time for you and your parents to consider a preparatory course before you take the test that counts. You should plan on taking the SAT (or the ACT, if that's what the colleges you are interested in prefer) more than once to get the best possible score. You also will be refining your goals in life and, with the help of your guidance counselor, tailoring your high school schedule to support those goals. These absolutely must include the "core" courses required if you are to receive an athletic scholarship at an NCAA school—three units of English, two of mathematics, two of social sciences, two of natural or physical sciences (including one lab course), and two units either from the above fields or of foreign language, computer science, philosophy or nondoctrinal religion.

Few students can accurately map out their futures at this point. But some patterns should have emerged. Maybe you have found you really like math and science after all. On the other hand, science courses may leave you cold while English literature fascinates you. You will be working with your guidance counselor to make the most of these new goals. While making sure you study all the fundamentals, you will add those advanced classes that fit in with your aims.

Just as your evolving athletic skills are determining your choice of schools, so should your career inclination. If you want to study science or engineering, you should take a harder look at colleges with strong programs in those fields. You also will be aware that lab courses take a lot of time, and so does sports practice. You'll have to start thinking about how best to balance these future demands on your time.

A warning: as you narrow your list of schools, you and your counselors should be aware of any special entrance requirements. Do you need two years of a foreign language?

Do you have to take achievement tests in certain subjects? It would be a shame to pick the perfect college—for both sports and academics—and then be turned down for admission because you are missing a course or a test.

THE ATHLETIC RESUMÈ—YOUR JUNIOR YEAR

Your junior year is when you should approach selected college coaches seriously. You will have been following some schools more closely than others, and your letter should reflect that familiarity. A call to make sure you have the right coach—there may have been a change—is a must. So is spelling his or her name correctly.

Appendix A to this book contains information and a model for a sports resumè. We think this is an excellent way to provide information to college personnel who are receiving hundreds of communications from prospective students. Some student-athletes begin using such resumès when writing for information in their sophomore years.

At the sophomore level, your cover letter should be a simple indication of interest. Closer to decision time, your letter should tell the coach why you are considering that college. Go beyond your interest in the sports program and explain how the school will help you realize your overall goals. You should also tell the coach how you think you could be an asset to her or his program. You should indicate you will need a scholarship or other financial aid and inquire about that availability.

Most importantly, you need a letter of recommendation from your high school coach. He or she should tell the college coach what you can contribute to the program. And that goes beyond physical skills, important as those are. Here is where to emphasize the intangibles—your work and practice habits, your sportsmanship, your inspiration to others on the team. We cannot stress too strongly the importance of this support from your coach in getting a college interested.

The college coach's response will necessarily be limited. She or he cannot phone you, accept a collect call from you or make personal contact with you before July 1 following your junior year (in Division I and Division II, the end of your junior year in Division III). But they can write you, and there's nothing to bar your talking to the coach while on an unofficial visit to the campus.

A caution: Many college coaches told us that high school coaches' letters often are sheer puffery. If the athlete were really that good she or he would already be in the Hall of Fame instead of looking for a college scholarship. Talk to your coach before he or she writes the letter. It should be as specific as possible—citing your accomplishments and potential—and realistic. Try to see that the coach does not paint a picture of you that your sports skills can't back up.

Your coach's role does not end with these letters. He or she will be the point person if and when you attract a college's interest. Your coach may get phone calls from the college coach (or an assistant) inquiring about your progress. Maintaining that interest, once expressed, is very important. Make sure your coach knows you appreciate the help you are getting.

What should you do if your high school coach changes jobs, and you are left with someone who's just met you for the first time? Use your former coach for a reference, by all means, but don't be afraid to talk to another coach in your area or conference—someone who has seen you play for a couple of years. They may be glad to help. Meanwhile, you should be establishing a relationship with your new coach.

Along with the letters and your athletic resumè, you might also include a transcript of your academic record up to that point. Be sure to keep the college coaches up-to-date on where and when you will be competing. And that means not only your regular high school schedule, but any summer league games or tournaments as well. The college coach may not drop by to see you personally, but he or she almost surely has some scouts out there.

FINAL PLAY—YOUR SENIOR YEAR

The summer between your junior and senior years is your last chance to showcase your skills at sports camps, clinics or in summer leagues. If a school high on your list has expressed interest and has a sports camp, you should attend if at all possible. Otherwise, you need your coach's advice and counsel on how to make this last shot an effective one.

Randy Lambert, athletic director and men's basketball coach at Division III Maryville College, prepared a list of suggestions for high school coaches to use in helping their athletes attract the attention of Division III sports staffs. Though no athletic scholarships are involved in Division III, a brief summary of them may give you a basis on which to judge what your own coach is doing to help you and your classmates:

Meet area Division III coaches, attend games, study their program and know the kind of athletes they need and want.

- Distribute an annual mail-out to Division III coaches about the senior athletes who are or may be valid prospects. Inform the interested coaches regularly through newsletter or phone calls about the prospect's seasonal progress.
- Keep a file on each senior athlete containing vital information.
- Work closely with the guidance office to supervise the athlete's academic performance.
- Make sure the athlete is completing the ACT and/or SAT tests in his or her junior year.
- Alert your senior athletes and check on their completion of the standardized financial aid forms.
- Have game films available or sent to college coaches.
- Maintain a checklist of your senior athletes' progress toward college admission. (Appendix B of this book)

ABOUT THOSE VIDEOS

More and more student-athletes are sending videotapes along with their letters. Almost all college coaches we talked with welcome tapes. But remember, coaches are busy people and will probably get hundreds of tapes to review. So keep yours short and to the point.

Tapes need not have Academy Award-winning cinematography, but they should be clear and sharp. All extraneous scenes should be edited out. They should not run more than five minutes. For team sports, include some "half-court" scenes, preferably from a high vantage point, showing how you move on the field and work with your teammates. You will also need some close-ups to show the fundamentals of your sport—hitting, throwing, running, stick-handling, whatever.

Another good tip from Coach Lambert. When sending game or meet videos, take nothing for granted. Be sure to include your uniform number (or other identifying mark) to avoid any possible confusion. Use standard VHS-format tapes.

Videos can be great, but they do not take the place of talent-indicating statistics and a strong recommendation from your coach. As a leading college golf coach noted, a video without some low scores and high tournament finishes is just another pretty picture. Another coach remembers a tape of a woman basketball player with her movements beautifully choreographed to classical music. She still remembers the tape—but isn't sure what happened to the player.

Coaches at your high school also might want to consider sponsoring an athletic "College Night," a plan that works successfully for Dan Meier, a football coach and guidance counselor in the Virginia suburbs of Washington, D.C. Coach Meier annually invites representatives from more than 65 colleges in his area to meet with senior men and women student-athletes from 40 high schools in December. This approach allows easy access to information for parents and students as application deadlines near.

Chapter 8
Tips for Campus Visits

Once you have a list of colleges that look like good matches for you, it's time to plan some visits.

Many of the questions that college athletic and academic personnel suggest you and your parents ask colleges may be done by telephone, of course. But nothing takes the place of getting the feel of the school for yourself.

REMEMBER THE RULES

There are some rules about visiting colleges that may or may not apply in your case. Your "official" expense-paid visit—in other words, the college is recruiting you—may not be made before you start classes in your senior year. You can make just one such visit to a school, and only five total official visits to NCAA Division I and Division II schools.

Beginning August 1, 1992, you may not make a official visit until you have supplied the school with the score you have made on one of the standardized tests—SAT, PSAT or ACT.

You may visit a college as many times as you wish, however, as long as you and your parents are picking up the tab. On those visits, the school can give you up to three complimentary tickets to an on-campus athletic event. In Division II and III, schools can also pay for one meal at an on-campus dining facility. But you and your parents cannot be "wined and dined." Even on the official visit there are some restrictions on how lavish the hospitality can be. Be aware of the rules (see Chapter 2). They are very specific and such seemingly trivial things as the gift of a cap or a T-shirt with the college logo have gotten schools, and the prospective student-athlete, in hot water.

Rules aside—and that doesn't mean to ignore or bend them—college visits are still the best way to judge a college and its athletic program.

This sounds like plain old common sense, and it is. But visiting schools at just the right time to do you the most good may be more of a problem than you first realize.

PLANNING YOUR VISIT

Ideally, you can learn a lot from going to a practice in your sport. Most importantly, you can watch the coach or coaches in action to see how they run the show. Can you take the "drill sergeant" approach? Screaming and yelling works fine for some students, but it's not everybody's style. Part of the reason for your visit is to eliminate as many unpleasant surprises as possible if you should attend a particular college.

So attending a practice is a fine idea, but it may be difficult. Your high school season and the college's may run at the same time—football, most definitely, but it's true for other sports as well.

Can you get away to make college visits? All the more reason to establish a good rapport with your high school coach. Ask her or him to work out a "game plan" that allows you to help the team while giving you time to visit colleges. That's another argument for an early start. Don't get caught in your senior year committing yourself to a college and a sports program about which you know almost nothing.

You may learn something very revealing in your first telephone call to a college. Don't be afraid to "trouble" someone with a call. If you find the people in the athletic department are too busy to talk to you, you may rightly decide that this isn't a place with students' interests in mind.

Chemistry—that certain "something"—is a big part of romance. It plays a part in your college selection, too. If all the factors are right, then nothing else is more important than your first-hand impression of a school. That's why visiting when the school is in session is so vital.

Talk to members of the team, though you have to be a little careful there. They are only human; they may or may not want to encourage you for reasons of their own—more competition for their positions, for instance. Still you need to check them out. You should be immediately suspicious, warns one leading coach, if the staff tries to steer you away from talking to players.

Don't limit your visits to the athletic field. Walk around, talk to other students. Find out about other aspects of student life. The athletic director of a small college in a small midwestern town advises prospective student-athletes to go to the cafeteria and talk to a variety of students (you might want to sample the cuisine). He pointed out since a small town doesn't usually have much to offer in the way of restaurants and cultural activities, you need to make sure a college in such a place provides enough facilities for social events to suit you.

If you are visiting a university, allow time to cover all the territory. Pick up copies of the university newspaper and any independent publications you find available.

ASK QUESTIONS

Now some specific questions that you and your parents should ask the athletic department before you make the decision to apply. We suggest you prepare a checklist of these questions so you can compare the answers you get from each college you visit.

1. How much time—both hours a day and months a year—will you be expected to spend on the practice field? Be sure the balance between sports time and class time is not going to put you in an academic bind. New NCAA rules restrict practice time to 20 hours a week, give student-athletes one day a week off, limit the hours that may be spent traveling to a from games and reduce the length of Division I and Division II seasons in all sports except football. Still, this may be more than you can afford to spend.

2. What support services are available? Are there study halls, independent counselors, tutors? Can you expect to pursue your chosen course of study and still have time for sports?

3. How many athletes graduate? What are the grade point averages on the team? Their majors? If all or most are physical education majors, are they being pushed in that direction?

4. Do athletes live in a special dorm or with the rest of the student body? Athletic dorms can be very well-outfitted, but they tend to put a wall between athletes and other students. The NCAA has directed its member schools to phase out athletic dorms over five years—by August 1, 1996. Training table meals also will be restricted to one a day during the regular academic year, also by August 1, 1996.

5. What happens if you get hurt? The NCAA won't let colleges give an ironclad promise that financial aid will continue, but what has the school's policy been? Ask for some examples of how injured athletes were treated.

6. How is the team shaping up for the years just ahead and how will you fit into the picture? Are there a host of other players at your position or do you fill a pressing need? How soon can you realistically expect to play?

7. Is the overall athletic program financially healthy? Is there any chance your sport could

be dropped entirely before you graduate? In some smaller schools, this is definitely not an off-the-wall question.

8. Are there any special weight restrictions that could be harmful to your health? Special diets have long been a problem in wrestling, but there have been recent problems in women's sports such as gymnastics and swimming. Finding out in advance can prevent serious problems later.

9. If your sport is considered a "minor" one at the college you are considering (you can hardly call lacrosse a minor sport if the team is its division's national champion, for instance), what are the qualifications of the coach? Is it his or her turn to coach (inwardly kicking and screaming) the volleyball team? Does the coach really know the game? Enough athletic directors mentioned this in interviews that it's worth your time to check.

10. This is even trickier, but try to find out if there is any chance the coach or any staff members in your sport are planning to leave. Some coaches seem to be on the list any time a college vacancy opens up, which should give you a signal. There are no guarantees, but occasionally this may save you some disappointment. A couple of sources for information might be the sports editors of the college or local newspapers.

Women student-athletes and their parents should certainly check out the school for its compliance with Title IX and stance toward women's sports.

The answers you get will help you in what may well become a juggling act. Big schools may have more support services for their athletes, but they may also demand more in terms of your time. Small schools, on the other hand, may offer fewer services but a closer relationship with your professors. The choices are difficult. But armed with all you have learned, now is the time to make the final cut—the list of several colleges where you feel comfortable both athletically and academically.

Chapter 9
Time to Decide

Now all the work you and the people helping you have done should pay off. Still, this can be an experience that makes memories of pulled teeth seem like the good old days.

If you have been going about choosing a college or university in the ways described in this book, you will have been making a list of prospects all along. Most important, you have faced reality and, without ruling out a "go for it" gamble, eliminated the impossible.

You know what you can do in your sport. You have an honest idea of what schools fit both your talent and desire. You have prepared your academic work and taken all the tests. You've been contacting coaches and working with your high school coach to get the attention of college athletic departments.

All the financial forms are done. Important note: Make copies of everything. A high school financial aid counselor tells horror stories of students whose forms were lost by colleges, and the students had no backups.

You've also visited some colleges. You have some dreams in your head about a few of them. Now it's time for some tough decisions.

WEDDING BELLS?

Remember, it takes two to make a marriage. You may have fallen in love with a particular school but found the feeling was not reciprocated. Admission and athletic department staffers may have been cordial and polite, but they were definitely lacking in passion.

Elsewhere, the situation may have been reversed. You were not impressed by the college and its programs, but its recruiters seem genuinely interested in you. What do you do?

For one thing, don't put all your hopes and dreams into one college application. By all means, apply to your first love, but give yourself some backups, too.

One top coach suggests you concentrate on three schools, plus a backup. Trying to compare more than that can only be confusing.

ASSESSING YOUR CHANCES

Even if you're not a blue-chipper, you may have gotten some sign of acceptance by college coaches. Try to pin this down as much as possible.

A coach who has been encouraging about your prospects may have been just as encouraging to dozens of others. Consider the coach's viewpoint. He or she has a need for players at particular positions to fill graduation vacancies or to shore up weak spots on the team. So do hundreds of other schools.

The coach may well have a short list of players he or she passionately wants. But just like you, coaches have to have some backups. It is to their advantage—although not always to yours—to keep as many prospects interested as they can until decision day.

The moral: Get something in writing if you can. Highly recruited athletes will surely be asked to sign a National Letter of Intent. Such letters are recognized by most of the major conferences and bind a player to a school. The player cannot back out without penalty. Signing dates vary with the sport, but always come after the end of that sport's season.

If you are not in the sought-after group, you may still be able to get some less-formal commitment from a college about admission and financial aid. In Division III schools, for example, no athletic letters of intent are permitted. But admission officers often write a letter to prospective students before the official notification date saying, in effect, we are holding a spot for you. So long as this is done for students generally—not just for athletes—it is perfectly within the rules.

Your coach and guidance counselor also may be talking to college coaches, admission people and financial aid officers. Their contacts should be helpful in evaluating your chances at a particular school.

THE APPLICATION AND FOLLOW-UP

So we come down to your formal application. Get the forms early and understand what is required. Some colleges ask for one or more essays. Don't wait until the last minute to start composing. Rewrite a couple of times. As with financial forms, make copies. Mail your application, along with recommendations from your counselors and a transcript of your grades, as early as possible.

Call the coaches you have been dealing with to let them know you have applied. In many Division III schools, for example, the coach has no formal role in the admission process. But there is nothing to stop her or him from inquiring whether your application has arrived. Such expressions of interest can often be helpful in moving your application into the "accepted" pile. A coach's interest also can help make sure your financial aid application does not get left on the sidelines.

THE DECISION

The Final Four of decisions comes after you hear from colleges. This can be a happy time if the news is good, and your "problem" is deciding between two or three equally attractive institutions.

Unfortunately, life also can be cruel. A desirable college may accept you for admission, but without any promise of an athletic scholarship or other financial aid. Your only offer may be from the college at the bottom of your list or—worst case scenario—no offers at all arrive in your mailbox. What do you do then?

Although all the schools you applied to should have some attraction, you still may have your heart set on your top choice. That is understandable. So do you go ahead and accept the offer of aid from the less-favored school anyway? That is a decision over which you, your parents and your advisers will have to agonize.

Lighten up a bit by talking to some of your friends who are in college. Chances are, those who didn't get into their first choice school are perfectly happy now and wonder why they wasted time being uptight.

There are some other options, of course.

You could attend a community college or junior college for a year or two and start the search for a scholarship all over again. Although this book concentrates on four-year colleges, junior colleges can have excellent sports programs—and also can be great places to flesh out your academic record.

If your family finances permit, you could go to the favored school that denied you a scholarship and take a swing at your sport as a walk-on. Many schools, especially the smaller ones, still encourage non-scholarship players to try out for the team. Perhaps if you prove yourself, a scholarship or other aid can be arranged for future years.

A wrong decision is not the end of the world, although you may have to pay some penalties. Athletes who sign a National Letter of Intent and then change their minds will lose, in almost all cases, two years of eligibility. So be sure before you sign anything.

Athletes who transfer from one four-year school to another lose no eligibility, but must sit out a year before they can start playing again.

College sports is a wide, wide world. We have concentrated on intercollegiate varsity sports, but in many ways they are just the tip of the athletic iceberg. Even if you do not get an athletic scholarship, and though you do not make a varsity team as a walk-on, your days on the playing fields need not be over.

Club sports are very popular in many schools. Although normally run by students and not by athletic departments (that's the rule in NCAA Division I schools), clubs can be very competitive. They play against other colleges and have good coaches. In a few rare cases, some offer financial aid.

If the school does not have club sports, you can always find intramurals. Most colleges have extensive programs in almost any sport you can name.

So here's to you and college sports, whichever way the ball may bounce!

Chapter 10
The Winning Edge

This book gives you ways to use your sport to help you obtain the best college education possible. That includes the fun of taking your sport to college and having a great time being part of college athletics.

But use your sport, don't be used by it, no matter what level of play or financial aid you can get from it.

If what looks like a great scholarship results in so much time spent playing big-time college sports that you don't graduate, you haven't ended up with much. A very small percentage of student-athletes make the pros, and of those, many have short careers. The cheering and the big money soon stop.

As Charles B. Reed, chancellor of the State University of Florida System, said in a speech at the NCAA annual meeting in January, 1989: "Your odds of becoming a rock star or an astronaut are about the same as starting for the New York Knicks."

Ollie Gelston, former basketball coach, now assistant athletics director at Montclair State College, a Division III school in New Jersey, says: "People say to me that to win is to be successful as a coach. Well, success to me is seeing my kids come back in a three-piece suit. That's success, that's coaching." Since 1959, 83 percent of Gelston's players have earned their degrees —going on to become doctors, dentists, lawyers, teachers and, yes, coaches.

And this attitude is not restricted to small colleges.

Penn State is a perennial football power. Coach Joe Paterno has earned an enviable reputation as both successful coach and teacher. Often asked which has been his best team, Coach Paterno says he cannot answer just yet. "Our best team will be the one that produces the most people who lead active, productive lives in our society," Paterno says.

Do the coaches you have been talking to understand the relationship of sports to the rest of your life? A few worn-out references at a sports awards banquet to "playing the game of life" is not what Coach Paterno is talking about. Don't settle for less. Fortunately, many coaches with Paterno's standards are out there, looking for student-athletes who want to work and learn.

"The Winning Edge" means many things. Information you find here may give you the winning edge on the path into college, but we hope that is not the end of it.

If taking time to research the right match for you and all your skills results in a satisfying college experience, that's a winning edge, too.

You will make lifelong friendships and take away memories of the Big Win over Wossamotta U. on club teams as well as the varsity. You can make lifelong friendships and take away memories of the Big Win over Phi Fratta Fratta on intramural teams. To the surprise of many athletes, you also can make lifelong friendships and take away memories of the Big Win over James Joyce's "Ulysses" in a college English classroom.

Although admission officers won't say so on the record, successful student-athletes have a bit of a winning edge in getting into some of the most selective graduate programs. Just as colleges are looking for "involved" students—musicians, student leaders and others as well as athletes—so are graduate schools. Your demonstrated ability to compete on the playing fields puts an added shine on your classroom performance.

Studies show that, except for the occasionally tragic conditions in big-time football and basketball, student-athletes have a higher graduation rate than the total school population.

Being on a team should teach you the importance of discipline, hard work, practice, taking responsibility for your own actions, giving up personal glory for the team good, how to win and how to lose; ingredients for success in any field.

Mike Mullan, an associate professor of physical education working on his doctorate in sociology, coaches men's tennis at Division III Swarthmore College and serves on the NCAA Men's and Women's Tennis Committee. Writing in the NCAA News, Mullan comments on the lessons sports can teach about society.

"Participation on a college sports team in the 1990s has some congruency with the way work is organized in our complex modern society," Mullan believes. "Players learn quickly that achievement in sports is not reducible to simple formulas—skill is a process that is guaranteed to be frustrating, with its many small successes and failures.

"In modern work, the way people get along is also important. On an individual level, the person who has learned to strive hard yet coexist with workers, who has the skills and disposition to pull together diverse sources of information and the ability to absorb temporary setbacks, has a leg up in an economy that stresses communications over production.

"At Swarthmore, over one-third of the student body plays a varsity sport. There are teams that experience championship moments and those whose records are sprinkled with more losses than wins; yet, I have to feel that all the students who play sports are learning implicit lessons about working in complex, modern organizations."

Yale University's sports brochures follow a "Path of Giants" theme, featuring not only on-field honors but the career and professional successes achieved by former team members as well.

Lifetime habits of exercise and nutrition can give you a real winning edge for years to come. More than one college refers to its "Life Sports" program. It's a rare college now that doesn't provide fitness equipment and training plus nutritional guidance for its athletes.

Juvenal, a Roman poet who lived in the first century A.D., wrote "Orandum est ut sit mens sana in corpore sano"—"You should pray for a sound mind in a sound body." That often-quoted phrase describes the completely educated person.

We've called it "The Winning Edge."

Section Two

Winning Teams and Coaches' Advice

BASEBALL

NCAA Division I champions: 1990-91, Louisiana State; 1989-90, Georgia; 1988-89, Wichita State; other past champions include Stanford, Arizona, Miami, Cal State Fullerton, Texas, Arizona State and Southern Cal.

NCAA Division II champions: 1990-91 and 1989-90, Jacksonville State; 1988-89, Cal Poly San Luis Obispo; other past champions include Florida Southern, Troy State, Cal State Northridge, Cal Poly Pomona and University of California Riverside.

NCAA Division III champions: 1990-91, Southern Maine; 1989-90, Eastern Connecticut State; 1988-89, North Carolina Wesleyan; other past champions include Ithaca, Montclair State, Marietta, Wisconsin-Oshkosh, and Ramapo.

NAIA champions: 1990-91, Lewis and Clark State (third title in a row).

PEOPLE ARE THE SECRET

from Gene Stephenson, Baseball Coach, Wichita State University

When visiting a college, the *people*—not the facilities—should be your foremost concern. Meet the people you are going to be around—players, coaches, instructors. Then ask yourself this question: Are they people with whom I want to spend the next four years of my life?

Getting ready to play college sports takes a lot of work. Summer leagues are a big help and so are sports camps. But, remember that the summer after your sophomore year is probably the earliest in terms of physical maturity. The summer after your junior year is when college coaches really start looking. If the college you have your eye on has a camp, attend it if at all possible. At least 25 percent of our players attended the Wichita State camp.

In evaluating your baseball skills, don't forget about the professional scouts. If one has seen you play, ask him—or have your coach ask him—at what level he thinks you can play. When contacting college coaches, be sure to tell them what scouts have seen you in action. And be sure the coach knows your schedule, summer league as well as regular season.

Be flexible in what you expect in a grant-in-aid. No baseball player at Wichita State in my years has ever been on a full scholarship—although I think all of them deserved one. Our College World Series champions, however, had 27 players receiving some aid. We re-examine scholarships every year and improve them to reflect the players' value to the team. So if an offer for your freshman year seems small, remember you'll have a chance to prove your worth.

Finally, work hard on all phases of your life by habit. By that I mean be the best you can be—by habit—in anything for which you are responsible. People who do that as a way of life are not faced with having to come up with a special effort in critical situations, they do it every day as a matter of habit.

Gene Stephenson's Shockers won the College World Series in 1989, were runners-up in 1991 and 1982 and finished third in 1988. He was named Coach of the Year in 1982.

BASKETBALL

MEN

NCAA Division I champions: 1990-91, Duke; 1989-90, University of Nevada-Las Vegas; 1988-89, Michigan; other past champions include Kansas, Indiana, Villanova, Georgetown, North Carolina State, North Carolina, Louisville, Michigan State, Kentucky, Marquette and UCLA (9 times).

NCAA Division II champions: 1990-91, University of North Alabama; 1989-90, Kentucky Wesleyan; 1988-89, North Carolina Central; other past champions include Lowell, Sacred Heart, Jacksonville State, Central Missouri State and Wright State.

NCAA Division III champions: 1990-91, University of Wisconsin-Platteville; 1989-90, Rochester; 1988-89, Wisconsin-Whitewater; other past champions include Ohio Wesleyan, North Park, Potsdam State, Scranton and Wabash.

NAIA champions: 1990-91, Oklahoma City; 1989-90, Birmingham-Southern; 1988-89, St. Mary's (TX).

WOMEN

NCAA Division I champions: 1990-91, Tennessee; 1989-90, Stanford; 1988-89, Tennessee; other past champions include Louisiana Tech, Texas, Old Dominion and Southern Cal.

NCAA Division II champions: 1990-91, North Dakota State; 1989-90 and 1988-89, Delta State; other past champions include Hampton, New Haven, Cal Poly Pomona, Central Missouri State and Virginia Union.

NCAA Division III champions: 1990-91, St. Thomas (MN); 1989-90, Hope; 1988-89, Elizabethtown; other past champions include Concordia-Moorhead, Wisconsin-Stevens Point, Salem State, Scranton, Rust and North Central.

NAIA champions: 1990-91, Fort Hays State; 1989-90, Southwestern Oklahoma; 1988-89, Southern Nazarene.

NEVER SAY "I WISH I HAD"

from Yvonne Kauffman, Women's Basketball Coach, Elizabethtown College

I have a motto I give to my teams: Never have to look at something and say "I wish I had." Be able to look back and say "I did."

That is as true for choosing a college and a sports program as it is for anything else in life. Do what feels right for you. If it doesn't work out and you are not happy, get out. There is nothing wrong with making a mistake so long as you do something to change it.

Of course you should not go into the selection process planning to make a mistake. There are some important steps you should take in making your choice. Make a checklist and rate all the schools on the same points.

First, visit the campus if at all possible. Meet the coach face to face. It really helps the coach to associate a face with a name. If you can't visit, a videotape is the next best thing. But keep it short. When your high school coach writes to recommend you, try to see that the letter accurately assesses your abilities. Too many are just puff. College coaches don't pay much attention to those.

Look at the academics first. You can only play basketball for four years, but your education is for life.

By all means watch the team play. Do you like the style of play? The uniforms? Is the coach a yeller and screamer or the quiet type? Could you play for her or him? Be wary of coaches who promise you too much.

Ask yourself what you really want. Do you need to be a star? A starter your first year? Or do you just want to be on a winning team? You should understand that if the team is in the playoffs regularly you may have to wait your turn to play. If being a star right away is more important, then you should look elsewhere. On the other hand, there are players who don't care that much about winning. They just want to be on a team. There are programs for them, too.

Finally, weigh the financial aid package carefully. It's great to be able to say you are on a basketball scholarship, but a need-based package at a Division III school could amount to more over your four years.

And then do what you have to do.

Yvonne Kauffman's Lady Jays were 1988-89 Division III national champions. They also won the national crown in 1982 and were in the finals in 1983 and 1984.

CREW

There is no official NCAA or NAIA championship in rowing, but the National Collegiate Rowing Championships are held annually in Cincinnati. Penn's varsity men's eight won in 1991, edging Northeastern by a foot or two. Boston University won the women's varsity eight crown. Others in the top tier of national crews are Harvard, Yale, Princeton, Pennsylvania, University of Wisconsin-Madison, Northeastern, Washington, Cornell, Stanford, Rutgers, Dartmouth and UCLA (cutting back to a club sport next year because of budgetary problems).

TAKE A HARD LOOK AT POTENTIAL, COMMITMENT

from Buzz Congram, Coach, Northeastern University

Prospective college rowers need to take a hard look at both their own potential and the level of commitment they want to make to the sport. That will make it easier to narrow down a choice of schools.

In comparison to other sports, there aren't a lot of crew programs. For those who want to row at the highest level there are the schools in the Eastern Association of Rowing Colleges (EARC) and a group on the West Coast that includes Washington, Cal Berkeley, UCLA and Stanford. Then there's the Dad Vail League, which has 30-40 schools with smaller programs. And don't forget the schools that have clubs only, if that matches your goals.

Almost all the EARC schools, with the exception of the Ivy League, have some money for rowers. It's not a lot—about the equivalent of two full scholarships in most cases. But it can be broken down into quite a few pieces.

Rowing is the kind of sport that relies not only on experienced athletes, but also on those who may have never rowed before. If an athlete has the size and physique, then we will take a chance on teaching the technique. I try to keep some money available for those as well, and to base aid on a combination of need and athletic ability.

Rowing coaches look for size—tall, not a lot of extra body weight—good numbers on ergometer (a sophisticated rowing machine) testing and desire. I rely heavily on the recommendations of high school coaches and rarely see a kid perform, except maybe on videos, which are most welcome. Serious high school rowers should think about trying out for the junior national team. That will involve some ergometer testing under controlled conditions and college coaches watch those carefully.

I don't have a big recruiting budget so I rely on letters I get from interested kids (just pick out several schools that seem to fit your needs and send a letter to the crew coach) and letters I write to coaches. I follow up with phone calls and, if there is mutual interest, we invite them for a campus visit.

Buzz Congram's Northeastern University crews are regularly ranked among the top in the country.

FIELD HOCKEY

NCAA Division I champions: 1990-91, Old Dominion University (fifth title in 10 years); 1989-90, North Carolina; 1988-89, Old Dominion; other past champions include Maryland, Iowa and Connecticut.

NCAA Division III champions: 1990-91, Trenton State (fifth title in 10 years); 1989-90, Lock Haven; 1988-89, Trenton State; other past champions include Bloomsburg, Salisbury State and Ithaca.

ASSERTIVENESS PAYS OFF

from Sharon Goldbrenner, Field Hockey and Women's Lacrosse Coach, Trenton State College

With hundreds of student-athletes striving to attract the attention of college coaches, you must highlight yourself so that a coach becomes familiar with your name and your face.

Make contact with coaches at schools in which you are interested during your junior year. Send them a letter, a good resume, a videotape.

Then, and this is extremely important, follow up with a phone call a week later. Don't stop there. Follow up with another call in the summer after your junior year and again early in your senior year.

Those student-athletes who are a little more assertive are the ones who come out on the high end. Coaches don't forget those who put out that extra effort.

As someone who coaches both field hockey and lacrosse, I definitely think women should try both sports. The basic skills are much the same. Although lacrosse is gaining in popularity, many field hockey players still come to college never having tried it. Then they try it, and it's like a fever. They love it.

For those who worry about balancing sports and classroom work, I find that 95 percent of my players—and I have a number who play both sports—do better academically during their sports seasons. They just seem to concentrate more.

There are many opportunities for woman athletes today. The most important thing is to take full advantage of them. Because if you don't, those same opportunities may not be available for the next generation of women athletes.

Sharon Goldbrenner has compiled a formidable record in her six seasons at Trenton State, winning three Division III national field hockey championships and three national lacrosse crowns. In 1990-91, she became the first Division III coach to win national championships in the two sports in the same academic year.

FOOTBALL

There is no playoff in NCAA Division IA. Instead, the "national champion" is selected by year-end polls of sportswriters by the Associated Press and of college coaches by United Press International. In 1990-91, Colorado and Georgia Tech tied, with Colorado leading the AP poll and Georgia Tech the UPI. (Beginning in the 1991-92 school year, the coaches' poll will be done by *USA Today*.)

NCAA Division IAA champions: 1990-91 and 1989-90, Georgia Southern (four titles in last six years); 1988-89, Furman; other past champions include Northeast Louisiana, Montana State, Southern Illinois, Eastern Kentucky, Idaho State and Boise State.

NCAA Division II champions: 1990-91, North Dakota State (fifth title in last eight years); 1989-90, Mississippi College; 1988-89, North Dakota State; other past champions include Troy State, Southwest Texas State, Cal Poly San Luis Obispo, Delaware and Eastern Illinois.

NCAA Division III champions: 1990-91, Allegheny; 1989-90, Dayton; 1988-89, Ithaca; other past champions include Augustana (four in a row from 1983-1986), Wagner, West Georgia, Widener and Baldwin-Wallace.

NAIA champions: Division I, 1990-91, 1989-90 and 1988-89, Carson-Newman; Division II, 1990-91, Peru State; 1989-90 and 1988-89, Westminster (PA).

DON'T SHORT-CHANGE YOURSELF

from Joe Paterno, Head Football Coach, Penn State University

Making a decision on what college or university to attend is one of the critical choices that confronts a young person—athlete or non-athlete.

Playing college sports and getting a quality education is no easy task. It's important the prospective student-athlete understand that in advance. At Penn State, we want our football players to excel on the athletic field. But we also want them to excel in the classroom and to be a part of the mainstream of campus life. If your prospective college doesn't want those things for you, maybe you should take a second look.

In the next four years, you are going to be asked to do some difficult things; to achieve some lofty goals. If you're serious about an education, you are going to have to work at establishing priorities. Plan to enjoy the entire college experience. Learn about art and literature and music and all of the things college has to offer. Don't confine your horizons to the locker room or the gymnasium. College should be a great time. It is the only time a person is really free.

Get to know the coaching staff and gain an appreciation not just for its knowledge of strategy but, every bit as important, the depth of its commitment to education. Does the institution offer academic support? Will academic excellence be expected and encouraged? Can you as an athlete expect to graduate at a rate consistent with the rest of the student body?

I want us to have a winning football team at Penn State because there is no sense being involved in something unless you want to be the best. But we are not going to sacrifice our academic credibility for the sake of a winning team, and you shouldn't either. People often ask me what our best team has been. I tell them I don't know yet. Our best team will be the one that produces the most people who lead active, productive lives in our society.

That should be a goal: A satisfying athletic experience, a meaningful college education and an active, productive life in society. If you settle for anything less, you are short-changing yourself.

Joe Paterno has been on the Penn State football staff more than 40 years and head coach for more than 25. His teams have won two national championships and made more than 20 bowl appearances. The graduation rate of his football players is annually among the tops in the country.

GOLF

MEN

NCAA Division I champions: 1990-91, Oklahoma State; 1989-90, Arizona; 1988-89, Oklahoma; other past champions include UCLA, Wake Forest, Houston and Brigham Young.

NCAA Division II champions: 1990-91 and 1989-90, Florida Southern (six titles in 12 years); 1988-89, Columbus; other past champions include Tampa, Troy State and Southwest Texas State.

NCAA Division III champions: 1990-91 and 1989-90, Methodist (NC); 1988-89, Cal State Stanislaus (six titles in a row, 12 in 15 years before moving up to Division II); other past champions include Allegheny, Ramapo and Wooster.

NAIA champions: 1990-91, Texas Wesleyan; 1989-90, Guilford (NC); 1988-89, Huntingdon (AL).

WOMEN

NCAA champions: 1990-91, UCLA; 1989-90, Arizona State; 1988-89, San Jose State; other past champions include Tulsa, Florida, Miami (FL) and Texas Christian.

HOW GOOD ARE YOU?

from Mike Holder, Men's Golf Coach, Oklahoma State University

Finding a team that matches your golf skills is a lot like finding a college that matches your academic skills. You have to be realistic.

How good are you? And what are your real goals? If you are not being heavily recruited, I'd advise staying close to home. I give in-state students preference, and I think most other coaches do the same.

There is one complication for golfers. If you live in one of the colder parts of the country, you may need to look south where we can play year-round.

How do you catch a coach's eye? Camps and tournaments, especially tournaments, are the places. If you are aiming at a nationally ranked school, then you need to be playing in national tournaments. If you are looking to a school in your state, then state tournaments are the ticket.

A lot of people are sending videos these days. But you better have something to back them up. If you can't show some low scores or high finishes in tournaments, then it doesn't matter what you look like on a video.

It is very important for you to find a program that offers you an opportunity to make the team. You will not improve if you do not get some tournament experience. A lot of great players have developed at smaller schools because they were given the opportunity to compete on a regular basis in tournaments.

Mike Holder's Oklahoma State Cowboys have been NCAA Division I national champions six times—in 1991, 1987, 1983, 1980, 1978, and 1976—and runners-up seven times. Players such as Bob Tway and Scott Verplank have gone on to the PGA tour.

ICE HOCKEY

NCAA Division I champions: 1990-91, Northern Michigan; 1989-90, University of Wisconsin; 1988-89, Harvard; other past winners include Lake Superior State, North Dakota, Michigan State, Rensselaer, Bowling Green, Minnesota and Boston University.

Division III champions: 1990-91, 1989-90 and 1988-89, University of Wisconsin-Stevens Point; other past champions, University of Wisconsin-River Falls, Plattsburgh State, Bemidji State, Rochester Institute of Technology and Babson College.

JUNIOR LEAGUES ATTRACT THE ATTENTION

from Mark Mazzoleni, Hockey Coach, University of Wisconsin-Stevens Point

One of the best ways to get the attention of college coaches is by playing Tier 2 junior hockey. Both the U.S. Junior Hockey League and the North American Junior Hockey League are closely scouted by coaches. You can play until you're 20, so many of the players have finished high school and are looking for the right college. The first priority of the junior leagues is to put kids into school.

For kids from parts of the country not known for hockey, the juniors offer a chance to show how good they are. You might score 100 goals and not get any notice if a coach knows the competition is weak. But players from hockey hotbeds can profit, too, from the increased competition of the juniors. They play 45-50 games a year, many more than high schools are permitted to play.

Another avenue is prep schools. Many of them have excellent hockey programs and they are geared to serve as feeders for Division III colleges in the East.

Above all, don't neglect the academics. It takes more than athletic skill to get into college. Your high school grades are important and you should take the entrance tests as many times as you can. Make personal contact with the schools in which you are interested to be sure you are taking the right high school courses and the right test—the ACT is favored in the Midwest, the SATs in the East. Entrance requirements are getting tougher all the time and it is up to you to be prepared.

Mark Mazzoleni's hockey team from University of Wisconsin-Stevens Point has won three NCAA Division III national championships in a row. In six seasons, his team has compiled a 138-52-10 record.

SKIING

MEN AND WOMEN

NCAA national champions: 1990-91, Colorado (10th title since 1970, 12th in all); 1989-90 and 1988-89, Vermont; other past champions include Utah (four titles between 1984 and 1988, six overall), Denver (14 titles in all, the last one in 1971), Wyoming and Dartmouth.

A POINT PROFILE IS A MUST

from Richard Rokos, Ski Coach, University of Colorado

Recruiting of skiers is at such a high level these days, internationally as well as nationally, that a high school skier must have a low point profile to even be considered for a scholarship.

You get a point profile by joining the United States Ski Association (the AFSI is the international equivalent) and participating in its meets. The earlier the better, because it takes a while to develop the kind of profile that college coaches pay attention to.

Every skier starts with 990 points and the goal is to get down as low as you can. A very talented skier should be down to 300 points the first year and to 100 the second. But from then on it gets very tough. The formula is very complicated, but the lower you get the harder it is to cut your numbers. Right now, the top colleges are looking for skiers whose profile is in the low teens.

Skiers who can't show the numbers needed to draw scholarship attention do have another approach. They can use a club team as a starting point to make the varsity. Here at Colorado we have more than 200 skiers involved on the club teams and developmental teams. Almost every year we have someone make it to the varsity from the club teams. These are usually skiers who didn't have impressive profile numbers, and who we hadn't seen. They used the club teams to show their abilities and work ethic.

Most colleges in snow country have club teams even if they don't have varsities. They offer wonderful competition for those who don't ski at the national or international level.

Richard Rokos' ski team won the NCAA national championship in 1990-91, his eighth season at Colorado.

SOCCER

MEN

NCAA Division I champions: 1990-91, UCLA; 1989-90, Virginia and Santa Clara (tie); 1988-89, Indiana (also won back-to-back titles in 1982 and 1983); other past champions include Clemson, Duke, Connecticut, San Francisco and SIU-Edwardsville.

NCAA Division II champions: 1990-91, Southern Connecticut State; 1989-90, New Hampshire College; 1988-89, Florida Tech; other past champions include Seattle Pacific, Florida International, Tampa, Lock Haven and Alabama A&M.

NCAA Division III champions: 1990-91, Glassboro State; 1989-90, Elizabethtown; 1988-89, UC San Diego; other past champions include North Carolina-Greensboro (five titles between 1982 and 1987), Wheaton, Babson and Lock Haven.

NAIA champions: 1990-91 and 1989-90, West Virginia Wesleyan; 1988-89, Sangamon State (Ill.).

WOMEN

NCAA Division I champions: 1990-91, North Carolina (fifth title in a row, eighth in tournament's nine years); George Mason (Va.) was champion in 1985-86; other top teams include North Carolina State, Massachusetts, Colorado College and Connecticut.

NCAA Division II champions: 1990-91, Sonoma State; 1989-90, Barry University; 1988-89, Cal State Hayward (first year for play-offs.)

NCAA Division III champions: 1990-91, Ithaca; 1989-90, UC San Diego; 1988-89, William Smith; other past champion, Rochester (1986 and 1987).

NAIA champions: 1990-91, Berry (GA); 1989-90 and 1988-89, Pacific Lutheran.

BEWARE OF BEING OVERSOLD

from Jerry Yeagley, Men's Soccer Coach, Indiana University

Your high school coach is an important player in your search for the right college. But sometimes coaches oversell a student-athlete's abilities. You may be the best player on your team and the coach—especially a volunteer or someone not familiar with the college scene—gets carried away.

How can you be sure you are getting a realistic appraisal of your talent? Here are some suggestions:

Watch college teams in which you are interested play—not once, but several times. Do you feel comfortable with the level of skills you see there? That's a very important sign.

Attend a summer camp where your abilities will be evaluated by college coaches. If you have your heart set on a particular school, by all means attend its camp. On our IU team, 11 of the 18 varsity players attended our summer camp. This should be the summer after your sophomore year at the very latest. Our top player at IU first came to camp when he was 12.

Try out for the best select soccer team you can. This can provide a good guide for you. If you don't make the team, then you may need to adjust your sights a bit lower. If you do, remember that college coaches follow the top select teams closely. A recommendation from a coach of one of these teams can make a real difference.

One other very important point: Before writing to a college coach, take the time to learn all you can about the coach and the program; how successful it is, how competitive. Your letter should show that this is a college you really want to attend and not just one of a score you are sending form letters to. A "Dear Coach" (no name) letter won't get you anywhere.

Jerry Yeagley's Hoosier soccer team won NCAA Division I national championships in 1988, 1983 and 1982. He has been named to the U.S. Soccer Federation's Hall of Fame.

SOFTBALL

NCAA Division I champions: 1990-91, Arizona; 1989-90, UCLA (third title in a row and sixth in nine years); other past champions include Texas A&M and Cal State Fullerton.

NCAA Division II champions: 1990-91, Augustana; 1989-90, Cal State Bakersfield (third title in a row); other past champions include Cal State Northridge (four titles between 1983 and 1987), Stephen F. Austin State and Sam Houston State.

NCAA Division III champions: 1990-91 and 1989-90, Eastern Connecticut State; 1988-89, Trenton State; other past champions include Central (IA) and Buena Vista.

NAIA champions: 1990-91, Hawaii-Loa; 1989-90, Kearney State (NE); 1988-89, Saginaw Valley.

SOME THINGS YOU CAN DO

from Susan Craig, Softball Coach, University of New Mexico

Finding the right college and/or an athletic scholarship is a real challenge. Here are some tips that may make things easier.

Start early. We like to watch athletes compete for a couple of years to get a good evaluation of their skills. Also, it's best to take the SAT or ACT tests more than once to get the best possible score.

Compete. Play at the highest level available. Also attend as many college camps or instructional schools as you can.

Educate yourself about the sport. Read everything available on your sport or position. Watch older youth teams or college games so you can see what skills are needed to play at that level. Keep up with the NCAA rankings. Write the sports information offices of colleges in which you are interested and ask for brochures, schedules and information on the teams' records and awards.

Get to know the coach. Talk to several former athletes, not just one. Talk to other coaches who deal regularly with that coach—one of your area youth coaches, for example. Visit the campus and watch the team practice and play. Learn all you can about the program's philosophy. Do they like to steal bases, hit and run, what do they do with runners at first and third?

Leaving or staying. Leaving home and being on your own is part of the growing-up process. But some athletes cannot deal with that and are better off attending a school close to home. Also, don't forget about the weather. There are good softball programs in all parts of the country, but you'll have more chances to play if you choose a college in one of the warmer areas.

Susan Craig started the successful University of New Mexico softball program 12 years ago. Considered one of the top teachers in the game, she is the author—with her co-head coach Ken Johnson—of The Softball Handbook.

SWIMMING AND DIVING

WOMEN

NCAA Division I champions: 1990-91, Texas (second title in a row, seventh in last eight years); 1988-89, Stanford; other champion, Florida (1982).

NCAA Division II champions: 1990-91 and 1989-90, Oakland; 1988-89, Cal State Northridge (third title in a row); other champions include Clarion and South Florida.

NCAA Division III champions: 1990-91, Kenyon (eighth title in a row); only other champion, Williams (1981-82 and 1982-83).

NAIA champions: 1990-91, Simon Fraser; 1989-90 and 1988-89, Puget Sound.

MEN

NCAA Division I champions: 1990-91, Texas (fourth title in a row); other past champions include Stanford, Florida, UCLA, California, Tennessee, Southern California and Indiana.

NCAA Division II champions: 1990-91, Cal State Bakersfield (sixth title in a row); other champions include Cal State Northridge (nine titles between 1975 and 1985), Oakland and Cal State Chico.

NCAA Division III champions: 1990-91, Kenyon (12th title in a row). Only other champions are Johns Hopkins (three titles between 1977 and 1979), St. Lawrence and Cal State Chico.

NAIA champions: 1990-91, Drury (third title in a row).

KEEP AN OPEN MIND

from Jim Steen, Swimming Coach, Kenyon College

Keeping an open mind is very important in choosing a college and a sports program. I see too many students who come to visit with a prejudice either for or against a school. One is as bad as the other.

Be an inquiring sort of person, but one who is receptive to being surprised or enlightened by what you see. Ask questions—of coaches, faculty, admissions people, students. And listen carefully to their answers.

Before you visit a school, you should have some idea that you would match up there both scholastically and athletically. Start with a personal letter—not a form letter—to the coach. Then check out all the information you receive and decide if you and the college could be a fit.

If the answer is yes, arrange a visit with the coach. If you are unsure about anything, ask. But you also must ask yourself what would satisfy you. Do you need just to be on a team or would you be happier somewhere else where you could be a starter? Get a direct commitment from the coach whenever possible about just what your role may be.

As you go through the selection process, you should narrow your focus to no more than four schools—three top choices and a backup. That's about all any person can give careful consideration to. And don't wait until the last minute to do the paperwork, especially the financial aid forms. Complete those even if you are not sure you are going to qualify.

As a coach, I play at most an indirect role in helping swimmers get into Kenyon. My real role is helping students decide if this is the place they really want and if they qualify. I want athletes to know they got in on their own merits.

Jim Steen's Kenyon swimmers have won an unprecedented 12 NCAA Division III men's national championships in a row as well as eight consecutive women's championships.

TENNIS

WOMEN

NCAA Division I champions: 1990-91, Stanford (sixth title in a row and eighth since 1982); Southern Cal won titles in 1983 and 1985; other top teams include Florida, UCLA, Miami (FL), Georgia and Trinity (TX).

NCAA Division II champions: 1990-91, Cal Poly Pomona; 1989-90, UC Davis; 1988-89, SIU-Edwardsville (fourth title in a row); other past champions are Tennessee-Chattanooga and Cal State Northridge.

NCAA Division III champions: 1990-91, Mary Washington; 1989-90, Gustavus Adolphus; 1988-89, UC San Diego; other past champions include Trenton State, Davidson, Principia and Occidental.

NAIA champions: 1990-91, Flagler (FL), (third title in a row).

MEN

NCAA Division I champions: 1990-91, Southern California; 1989-90, Stanford (third title in a row and 11th since 1973); other past champions include Georgia and UCLA.

NCAA Division II champions: 1990-91, Rollins; 1989-90, Cal Poly San Luis Obispo; 1988-89, Hampton; other past champions include Chapman, SIU-Edwardsville and UC Irvine.

NCAA Division III champions: 1990-91, Kalamazoo; 1989-90, Swarthmore; 1988-89, UC Santa Cruz; other past champions include Washington and Lee, Redlands and Gustavus Adolphus.

NAIA champions: 1990-91, Lander (SC); 1989-90, Elon (NC); 1988-89, Texas-Tyler.

GET SOME TOURNAMENT EXPERIENCE

from Bob Meyers, Former Women's Tennis Coach,
Southern Illinois University-Edwardsville

If you hope to play tennis on a college team—especially at a Division I or Division II school—you need to get all the experience you can. And that doesn't mean just in high school matches.

Play in as many tournaments as you possibly can—at the highest level you can qualify for. This will get you a United States Tennis Association ranking and that's something that means a lot to college coaches. They are looking for mature players with a lot of experience. And the rankings help them pick and choose. As a Division II coach, I looked for players ranked No. 70 or above on a national scale. Other schools have their own standards.

I received letters from hundreds of tennis players who were interested in my team. Unfortunately, most of those letters didn't tell me much about the player's skill level. If you are sending an athletic resume to a coach, be as specific as possible. Tell him or her what tournaments you have played in, who you played against and the scores. The coach may know nothing about you, but he or she may recognize your opponent's name. Even a loss in a close match says something about your game. The more you can tell a coach about your skills the better chance you will have.

For good high school players who are not ranked and who aren't being recruited by a Division I or II school, the best choice may well be a Division III college. That means no athletic scholarship, but other financial aid may amount to just about as much. A player who blossoms in Division III can always transfer to a higher-ranked school.

Of course, you can always be a walk-on and try to make a team that hasn't recruited you. But you have to realize you'll be up against players with a lot of experience. College sports should be fun, not something that overwhelms you. Picking the proper level at which to play can make it both competitive and fun.

Bob Meyers' Southern Illinois University-Edwardville teams won four straight NCAA Division II national women's titles from 1986 to 1989. He retired from coaching after the 1989 season.

TRACK AND FIELD/CROSS COUNTRY

CROSS COUNTRY

MEN

NCAA Division I champions: 1990-91, Arkansas (won 4 of last 7 titles); 1989-90, Iowa State; 1988-89, Wisconsin; other past champions include University of Texas-El Paso, Oregon and Tennessee.

NCAA Division II champions: 1990-91, Edinboro; 1989-90, South Dakota State; 1988-89, Edinboro and Mankato State (tie); other past champions include Southeast Missouri State, Cal Poly Pomona, Eastern Washington, Millersville and Humboldt State.

NCAA Division III champions: 1990-91, 1989-90 and 1988-89 University of Wisconsin-Oshkosh; other past champions include North Central, St. Thomas (MN), Luther and Brandeis.

WOMEN

NCAA Division I champions: 1990-91 and 1989-90, Villanova; 1988-89, Kentucky; other past champions include Oregon, Texas, Wisconsin and Virginia.

NCAA Division II champions: 1990-91, Cal Poly San Luis Obispo, its ninth title in a row; only other champion is South Dakota State (1981).

NCAA Division III champions: 1990-91 and 1989-90, Cortland State; 1988-89, University of Wisconsin-Oshkosh; other champions include St. Thomas (MN), Franklin and Marshall, Wisconsin-LaCrosse and Central (IA).

TRACK AND FIELD

WOMEN'S INDOOR

NCAA Division I champions: 1990-91, Louisiana State; 1989-90, Texas; 1988-89, Louisiana State; other past champions include Florida State and Nebraska.

NCAA Division II champions: 1990-91, Abilene Christian (fourth title in a row); St. Augustine's has won two titles.

NCAA Division III champions: 1990-91, Cortland State; 1989-90, 1988-89 and 1987-88, Christopher Newport. University of Massachusetts-Boston also won three in a row (1985-87).

NAIA champions: 1990-91, Prairie View; 1989-90, Simon Fraser; 1988-89, Midland Lutheran.

MEN'S INDOOR

NCAA Division I champions: 1990-91, Arkansas (eighth title in a row); other past champions include Southern Methodist, University of Texas-El Paso, Villanova and Washington State.

NCAA Division II champions: 1990-91, St. Augustine's (fifth title in a row); Abilene Christian tied for the title in 1987-88 and Southeast Missouri State won in 1984-85.

NCAA Division III champions: 1990-91, Wisconsin-LaCrosse; 1989-90, Lincoln (PA); 1988-89, North Central. Other past champions were Frostburg State and St. Thomas (MN).

NAIA champions: 1990-91, Lubbock Christian; 1989-90, Adams State; 1988-89, Wayland Baptist.

WOMEN'S OUTDOOR

NCAA Division I champions: 1990-91, Louisiana State (fifth title in a row); other past champions include Texas, Oregon, Florida State and UCLA.

NCAA Division II champions: 1990-91, Cal Poly San Luis Obispo (third title in a row). Other champion, Abilene Christian (four straight titles from 1985 to 1988).

NCAA Division III champions: 1990-91 and 1989-90, Wisconsin- Oshkosh; 1988-89, Christopher Newport (third title in a row); other past champions include University of Massachusetts-Boston, Cortland State, Wisconsin-LaCrosse and Central (IA).

NAIA champions: 1990-91, Central State (Ohio); 1989-90 and 1988-89, Prairie View (TX).

MEN'S OUTDOOR

NCAA Division I champions: 1990-91, Tennessee; 1989-90 and 1988-89, Louisiana State; other past champions include UCLA, Southern Methodist, Southern Cal, Arkansas, Oregon and University of Texas-El Paso.

NCAA Division II champions: 1990-91, St. Augustine's (third title in a row); other past champions include Texas Christian (seven straight titles between 1982 and 1988), Cal Poly San Luis Obispo, Cal State Los Angeles and Cal State Hayward.

NCAA Division III champions: 1990-91, Wisconsin-LaCrosse; 1989- 90, Lincoln (PA); 1988-89, North Central; other past champions include Frostburg State, Glassboro State (five straight titles between 1980 and 1984) and Slippery Rock.

NAIA champions: 1990-91, Oklahoma Baptist; 1989-90 and 1988-89, Azusa Pacific.

EXPLORE ALL THE POSSIBILITIES

from Wes Kittley, Women's Track Coach, Abilene Christian University

I am constantly surprised at the amount of financial aid available to students—and that doesn't mean just student- athletes.

The aid is there; you just have to look for it. As a Division II coach, the athletic scholarships I can give are limited. Many of the young athletes I recruit will get no athletic scholarships at all. That's where the other possibilities come in.

Visit the campus with your parents and talk to the financial aid office. Have family income figures ready. You will probably be pleasantly surprised. There are academic scholarships, ethnic and other special scholarships, Pell Grants, state grants, matching grants and many more. You may well come up with a package that goes a long way toward paying the cost of your college education. Start looking at what is available during your junior year in high school for best results.

As a track coach, I have an advantage over coaches in some other sports. I get periodic reports on the best times and distances in many states. Yet there are many borderline athletes who could help my team that I never hear about. By all means, write the coaches at schools you are interested in and let them know about you—not just your sports skills, either, but about you as a student and as a person.

Videotapes can be useful, too, but keep them short. If the school you have your eye on has a summer camp, that's a good place to catch the coach's eye.

It is getting harder and harder for smaller schools to get the real blue-chip athletes. But we all need good student-athletes and that could be you. So let us coaches know you are out there.

Wes Kittley's track team has won four national Division II women's indoor titles in a row, as well as outdoor crowns in 1985, 1986, 1987 and 1988.

VOLLEYBALL

WOMEN

NCAA Division I champions: 1990-91, UCLA; 1989-90, Long Beach State; 1988-89, Texas; other past champions include Hawaii, Pacific and Southern Cal.

NCAA Division II champions: 1990-91, West Texas State; 1989-90, Cal State Bakersfield; 1988-89, Portland State (third title in eight years); other past champions include Cal State Northridge, UC Riverside and Cal State Sacramento.

NCAA Division III champions: 1990-91, UC San Diego (fourth title in five years); 1989-90, Washington University (MO); other past champions are Elmhurst and La Verne.

NAIA champions: 1990-91, Hawaii Pacific; 1989-90, Fresno Pacific; 1988-89, Hawaii-Hilo.

MEN

NCAA national champions: 1990-91, Long Beach State; 1989-90, Southern Cal (fourth title); 1988-89, UCLA (13th title in 20 years); other past champions are Pepperdine (three titles) and San Diego State.

DON'T LET SIZE SCARE YOU AWAY

from Mick Haley, Women's Volleyball Coach, University of Texas

High school kids do some crazy things in the process of picking a college. One is to let the size of a school scare them off without ever finding out how that size can work in their favor.

Major athletic programs—the good ones—have tremendous resources. Many provide academic coaches, study halls, counseling programs. Still, some students will choose a small school without understanding that its athletic program may be on a shoestring budget, and they will be left to work out their own problems.

Bigness is no guarantee, however. Athletes, especially women, should ask some tough questions about the kind of support they can expect. For example:

* What percentage of student-athletes graduate? I would find it scary if the figure for all athletes is not in the 60th percentile. What percent of athletes who complete their eligibility graduate? That figure should be in the 90s.
* What is the GPA of the team? What are their majors? If they are all in PE, are they being guided that way?
* Is there a study hall program? Can you get help in how to study? Are tutors available? Enough tutors? Who pays for them?
* Is there a rehabilitation department to help you come back from an injury? How does the school handle career-ending injury? Is there a nutrition program, and does the school require you to establish a certain weight? Is there drug education? An independent counseling program, and is it aimed at help you or helping the team?

It is vitally important that you watch games and practices to check out the coach's style. Some athletes do their best when being screamed at. Others don't. Some high school kids seem to have a self-destructive streak in picking a coaching style that is totally wrong for them. Don't you make the same mistake!

Mick Haley's team won the 1988-89 NCAA Division I championship, becoming the first team outside of California or Hawaii to take a national volleyball crown. It also was the first team to go undefeated in the national tournament.

OTHER SPORTS

FENCING

MEN AND WOMEN

NCAA national champions: 1990-91 and 1989-90, Penn State.

WOMEN

NCAA national champions: 1988-89, Wayne State (second straight title); other past champions include Notre Dame, Pennsylvania and Yale.

MEN

NCAA national champions: 1988-89, Columbia (third straight title); other past champions include Notre Dame, Wayne State, Pennslyvania and New York University.

GYMNASTICS

WOMEN

NCAA national champions: 1990-91, Alabama (also won in 1987- 88); 1989-90, Utah (sixth title since 1982); 1988-89, Georgia (second title in three years).

MEN

NCAA national champions: 1990-91, Oklahoma; 1989-90, Nebraska (seventh title); 1988-89, Illinois (ninth title, but first since 1958); other past champions include Penn State (nine titles), UCLA, Arizona State, Ohio State, Indiana State, California, Iowa State and Southern Illinois.

RIFLE

MEN AND WOMEN

NCAA national champions: 1990-91, West Virginia (fourth title in a row and seventh since 1983); other past champions are Murray State and Tennessee Tech.

WATER POLO

NCAA national champions: 1990-91, California (third title in last four years); 1989-90, UC Irvine; other past champions are Stanford, UC Santa Barbara and UCLA.

WRESTLING

NCAA Division I champions: 1990-91, Iowa (12th title since 1975, including nine in a row between 1978 and 1986); 1989-90, Oklahoma State (second title in a row, 29th overall); other past champions include Arizona State, Iowa State and Oklahoma.

NCAA Division II champions: 1990-91, Nebraska-Omaha; 1989-90 and 1988-89, Portland State; other past champions include North Dakota State, SIU-Edwardsville, Cal State Bakersfield, Northern Iowa and Cal Poly San Luis Obispo.

NCAA Division III champions: 1990-91, Augsburg (MN); 1989- 90 and 1988-89, Ithaca; other past champions include St. Lawrence, Trenton State, Montclair State and Brockport State.

NAIA champions: 1990-91, Northern Montana; 1989-90, Adams State; 1988-89, Central State (OK).

Section Three

NCAA, Division IA

These are the big football schools—I-A being a football-only classification. They are the ones you see on TV on Saturday afternoons and in the bowl games. There is no NCAA play-off in this division, the "national champion" being crowned on the basis of year-end rankings in the Associated Press poll of sportswriters and United Press International poll of college coaches. (Beginning in the 1991-92 school year, the coaches' poll will be done by USA Today.) The NCAA requires that Division I-A schools have stadiums that seat at least 30,000, and home attendance must average 17,000. Division I-A schools must field varsity teams in seven men's or mixed team sports and seven women's sports. All offer football scholarships.

The graduation rate information listed here was provided voluntarily by the schools to the Chronicle of Higher Education. Legislation to require such reporting is still pending in Congress.

The abbreviation D/R represents "Declined to Respond." The abbreviation N/A represents "Not Available." W/held stands for "Withheld."

PERCENTAGE GRADUATING BY 1989

	'84 freshman	'84 freshman athletes	male athletes	female athletes	'84 football recruits	'84 men's basketball recruits
ALABAMA						
Auburn University Auburn, AL 36849 (205) 844-4750	56.2	42.2	30.2	63.3	14.8	0.0
University of Alabama Tuscaloosa, AL 35487 (205) 348-3697	42.3	32.7	25.0	52.9	20.0	0.0
ARIZONA						
Arizona State University Tempe, AZ 85287 (602) 965-3482	37.6	30.5	21.8	48.1	27.3	33.3
University of Arizona Tucson, AZ 85721 (602) 621-2200	36.0	43.9	W/held	W/held	W/held	W/held
ARKANSAS						
University of Arkansas Fayetteville, AR 72701 (501) 575-3753	32.3	34.0	34.0	45.8	42.9	33.3
CALIFORNIA						
California State University Fresno, CA 93740 (209) 278-2324	31.0	29.3	25.0	36.4	25.0	33.3

60

	'84 freshman	'84 freshman athletes	male athletes	female athletes	'84 football recruits	'84 men's basketball recruits
California State University Fullerton, CA 92634 (714) 773-3456	27.4	23.9	19.2	40.0	8.3	0.0
California State University Long Beach, CA 90840 (213) 985-4655	17.5	29.5	28.1	33.3	57.1	12.5
San Diego State University San Diego, CA 92182 (619) 594-5162	22.1	15.8	15.8	15.8	W/held	W/held
San Jose State University San Jose, CA 95192 (408) 924-1200	D/R					
Stanford University Stanford, CA 94305 (415) 723-1413	88.8	84.1	82.9	86.4	71.4	66.7
University of California Berkeley, CA 94720 (415) 642-5316	65.0	62.4	54.5	73.2	51.6	33.3
University of California Los Angeles, CA 90024 (213) 825-8699	62.6	54.6	51.0	61.1	50.0	33.3
University of the Pacific Stockton, CA 95211 (209) 946-2248	48.7	64.0	62.1	66.7	50.0	40.0
University of Southern California Los Angeles, CA 90089 (213) 743-2221	53.5	46.6	39.5	56.7	25.0	100.0

COLORADO

	'84 freshman	'84 freshman athletes	male athletes	female athletes	'84 football recruits	'84 men's basketball recruits
Colorado State University Fort Collins, CO 80523 (303) 491-5300	50.3	65.0	66.7	61.5	70.0	66.7
University of Colorado Boulder, CO 80309 (303) 492-7931	56.1	53.7	59.1	30.0	51.9	33.3
U.S. Air Force Academy USAF Academy, CO 80840 (719) 472-4008	D/R					

FLORIDA

	'84 freshman	'84 freshman athletes	male athletes	female athletes	'84 football recruits	'84 men's basketball recruits
Florida State University Tallahassee, FL 32306 (904) 644-1060	47.4	40.5	34.0	57.1	36.4	50.0

61

PERCENTAGE GRADUATING BY 1989

	'84 freshman	'84 freshman athletes	male athletes	female athletes	'84 football recruits	'84 men's basketball recruits
University of Miami Coral Gables, FL 33124 (305) 284-3822	D/R					
University of Florida Gainesville, FL 32604 (904) 375-4683	47.5	33.8	25.5	52.2	29.6	20.0
GEORGIA						
Georgia Institute of Technology Atlanta, GA 30332 (404) 894-5411	57.3	56.1	54.2	66.7	55.0	25.0
University of Georgia Athens, GA 30613 (404) 542-1307	57.2	36.5	33.3	41.2	32.1	0.0
HAWAII						
University of Hawaii Honolulu, HI 96822 (808) 956-7301	71.6	73.8	69.0	82.6	77.8	n/a
ILLINOIS						
Northern Illinois University DeKalb, IL 60115 (815) 753-0888	48.4	48.4	44.4	57.1	55.0	28.6
Northwestern University Evanston, IL 60208 (708) 491-8880	86.0	84.7	83.6	88.2	81.5	100.0
University of Illinois Champaign, IL 61820 (217) 333-3678	76.2	64.6	62.0	71.4	52.4	25.0
INDIANA						
Ball State University Muncie, IN 47306 (317) 285-8225	55.0	80.2	75.0	89.3	58.8	75.0
Indiana University Bloomington, IN 47405 (812) 855-1966	57.6	53.8	54.4	52.0	56.0	66.7
Purdue University Lafayette, IN 47907 (317) 494-3189	66.7	62.8	58.8	73.1	40.7	60.0

	'84 freshman	'84 freshman athletes	male athletes	female athletes	'84 football recruits	'84 men's basketball recruits
University of Notre Dame Notre Dame, IN 46556 (219) 239-6107	92.7	92.8	91.2	100.0	81.3	75.0
IOWA						
Iowa State University Ames, IA 50011 (515) 294-3662	54.6	46.8	32.8	69.4	26.7	0.0
University of Iowa Iowa City, IA 52242 (319) 335-9435	55.4	61.1	59.0	64.7	56.7	33.3
KANSAS						
Kansas State University Manhattan, KS 66506 (913) 532-6910	41.7	46.5	41.9	58.3	47.4	100.00
University of Kansas Lawrence, KS 66045 (913) 864-3143	47.0	54.4	46.7	65.1	52.4	28.6
KENTUCKY						
University of Kentucky Lexington, KY 40506 (606) 257-8000	48.4	38.5	39.0	37.5	45.5	20.0
University of Louisville Louisville, KY 40292 (502) 588-5732	22.2	40.4	32.5	58.8	18.8	0.0
LOUISIANA						
Louisiana State University Baton Rouge, LA 70803 (504) 388-3600	25.9	24.1	23.4	25.6	21.4	16.7
Louisiana Tech University Ruston, LA 71272 (318) 257-4111	34.2	36.1	30.0	63.6	33.3	
Tulane University New Orleans, LA 70118 (504) 865-5502	D/R					
Univ. of Southwestern Louisiana Lafayette, LA 70506 (318) 231-6318	22.7	19.5	22.6	10.0	21.1	0.0

PERCENTAGE GRADUATING BY 1989

	'84 freshman	'84 freshman athletes	male athletes	female athletes	'84 football recruits	'84 men's basketball recruits
MARYLAND						
United States Naval Academy Annapolis, MD 21402 (301) 267-2429	75.4	66.8	66.8	none enrolled	85.2	55.6
University of Maryland College Park, MD 20740 (301) 454-4705	50.2	49.4	41.1	69.6	11.1	0.0
MASSACHUSETTS						
Boston College Chestnut Hill, MA 02167 (617) 552-4681	85.1	89.4	82.4	97.7	85.0	100.0
MICHIGAN						
Central Michigan University Mount Pleasant, MI 48859 (517) 774-3046	46.7	58.6	54.9	64.4	51.7	20.0
Eastern Michigan University Ypsilanti, MI 48197 (313) 487-1050	24.9	33.3	31.5	38.7	23.5	0.0
Michigan State University East Lansing, MI 48824 (517) 355-1623	59.7	60.8	55.6	75.0	44.0	75.0
University of Michigan Ann Arbor, MI 48109 (313) 764-6227	76.5	60.6	54.9	77.8	56.8	0.0
Western Michigan University Kalamazoo, MI 49008 (616) 387-3120	36.5	48.7	49.1	47.6	40.7	66.7
MINNESOTA						
University of Minnesota Minneapolis, MN 55455 (612) 625-9579	27.0	36.0	24.7	59.5	21.4	25.0
MISSISSIPPI						
Mississippi State University Mississippi State, MS 39762 (601) 325-2532	45.5	37.7	39.2	33.3	33.3	25.0
University of Mississippi University, MS 38677 (601) 232-7241	48.0	34.5	33.3	40.0	37.5	20.0

	'84 freshman	'84 freshman athletes	male athletes	female athletes	'84 football recruits	'84 men's basketball recruits
University of Southern Mississippi Hattiesburg, MS 39406 (601) 266-5017	35.6	30.0	28.1	66.7	29.2	16.7
MISSOURI						
University of Missouri Columbia, MO 65211 (314) 254-6641	46.7	46.3	40.4	54.3	35.3	50.0
NEBRASKA						
University of Nebraska Lincoln, NE 68588 (402) 472-3644	42.0	39.9	36.2	50.0	41.2	100.0
NEVADA						
University of Nevada Las Vegas, NV 89154 (702) 739-3983	20.8	21.1	14.3	40.0	17.4	0.0
NEW JERSEY						
Rutgers University New Brunswick, NJ 08903 (201) 932-8610	67.7	73.9	71.7	77.6	84.2	n/a
NEW MEXICO						
New Mexico State University Las Cruces, NM 88003 (505) 646-1211	31.0	34.7	28.1	60.0	20.8	25.0
University of New Mexico Albuquerque, NM 87131 (505) 277-6375	13.6	25.3	20.0	36.7	24.0	0.0
NEW YORK						
Syracuse University Syracuse, NY 13244 (315) 443-2385	62.1	67.8	63.5	77.8	68.2	33.3
United States Military Academy West Point, NY 10996 (914) 938-3701	75.4	66.8	66.8	none enrolled	63.2	45.5

PERCENTAGE GRADUATING BY 1989

	'84 freshman	'84 freshman athletes	male athletes	female athletes	'84 football recruits	'84 men's basketball recruits
NORTH CAROLINA						
Duke University Durham, NC 27706 (919) 684-2431	92.3	95.9	96.1	95.0	92.3	100.0
East Carolina University Greenville, NC 27858 (919) 757-4501	38.3	42.0	39.6	47.6	50.0	0.0
North Carolina State University Raleigh, NC 27695 (919) 737-2109	51.1	50.4	40.9	71.8	27.8	25.0
University of North Carolina Chapel Hill, NC 27514 (919) 962-6000	72.2	70.7	68.1	76.2	71.4	50.0
Wake Forest University Winston-Salem, NC 27109 (919) 759-5616	78.7	63.2	56.9	100.0	40.0	0.0
OHIO						
Bowling Green State University Bowling Green, OH 43403 (419) 372-2401	54.6	52.6	45.8	63.9	31.6	25.0
Kent State University Kent, OH 44242 (216) 672-3120	36.3	44.0	42.9	46.2	42.9	0.0
Miami University Oxford, OH 45056 (513) 529-3108	73.1	67.4	62.1	79.3	50.0	57.1
Ohio State University Columbus, OH 43210 (614) 292-7572	46.2	52.9	47.4	61.7	21.7	25.0
Ohio University Athens, OH 45701 (614) 593-1174	51.6	59.5	53.0	70.8	43.3	50.0
University of Akron Akron, OH 44325 (216) 972-7080	28.5	52.1	51.0	55.0	39.1	n/a
University of Cincinnati Cincinnati, OH 45221 (513) 556-2330	40.6	39.8	35.6	47.1	36.4	0.0
University of Toledo Toledo, OH 43606 (419) 537-4987	31.0	30.8	32.3	28.6	28.6	25.0

	'84 freshman	'84 freshman athletes	male athletes	female athletes	'84 football recruits	'84 men's basketball recruits
OKLAHOMA						
Oklahoma State University Stillwater, OK 74078 (405) 744-5733	37.6	27.5	25.0	36.4	28.0	0.0
University of Oklahoma Norman, OK 73019 (405) 325-8200	35.0	27.1	22.8	39.3	25.0	0.0
University of Tulsa Tulsa, OK 74104 (504) 865-5502	46.4	50.9	43.9	71.4	41.7	25.0
OREGON						
Oregon State University Corvallis, OR 97331 (503) 737-2547	26.3	28.1	21.7	44.4	31.6	16.7
University of Oregon Eugene, OR 97403 (503) 346-5464	44.2	50.0	46.0	55.3	40.0	66.7
PENNSYLVANIA						
Pennsylvania State University University Park, PA 16802 (814) 865-1086	D/R					
Temple University Philadelphia, PA 19122 (215) 787-7447	D/R					
University of Pittsburgh Pittsburgh, PA 15904 (412) 648-8230	D/R					
SOUTH CAROLINA						
Clemson University Clemson, SC 29631 (803) 656-2218	66.5	51.6	47.8	62.5	60.0	33.3
University of South Carolina Columbia, SC 29208 (803) 777-4202	57.0	58.9	51.5	77.8	36.7	0.0
TENNESSEE						
Memphis State University Memphis, TN 38152 (901) 678-2335	16.2	32.7	35.7	23.1	26.3	33.3

PERCENTAGE GRADUATING BY 1989

	'84 freshman	'84 freshman athletes	male athletes	female athletes	'84 football recruits	'84 men's basketball recruits
University of Tennessee Knoxville, TN 37996 (615) 974-1224	42.8	29.5	20.8	56.5	16.7	20.0
Vanderbilt University Nashville, TN 37212 (615) 322-4831	75.9	71.7	68.2	88.9	69.0	0.0
TEXAS						
Baylor University Waco, TX 76798 (817) 754-4648	64.0	52.4	50.0	60.0	64.7	0.0
Rice University Houston, TX 77251 (713) 527-9851	81.8	70.1	65.3	83.3	69.6	66.7
Southern Methodist University Dallas, TX 75275 (214) 692-4301	67.3	41.8	34.0	64.7	16.0	60.0
Texas A&M University College Station, TX 77843 (409) 845-2227	58.9	24.7	24.2	26.3	6.7	0.0
Texas Christian University Fort Worth, TX 76129 (817) 921-7965	52.9	53.8	53.3	55.0	48.4	25.0
Texas Tech University Lubbock, TX 79409 (806) 742-3355	33.8	39.2	28.6	72.2	15.4	0.0
University of Houston Houston, TX 77204 (713) 749-3722	19.5	18.1	12.5	36.8	20.0	0.0
University of Texas at Austin Austin, TX 78712 (512) 471-5757	52.0	42.3	27.7	71.9	28.0	0.0
University of Texas at El Paso El Paso, TX 79968 (915) 747-5347	13.9	22.5	20.7	27.3	16.7	0.0
UTAH						
Brigham Young University Provo, UT 84602 (801) 378-6164	D/R					
University of Utah Salt Lake City, UT 84112 (801) 581-5605	D/R					

	'84 freshman	'84 freshman athletes	male athletes	female athletes	'84 football recruits	'84 men's basketball recruits
Utah State University Logan, UT 84322 (801) 750-1862	D/R					
VIRGINIA						
University of Virginia Charlottesville, VA 22903 (804) 982-5100	89.3	86.0	31.3	100.0	81.5	40.0
Virginia Polytechnic Institute Blacksburg, VA 24061 (703) 231-6796	66.7	55.1	48.2	81.8	19.0	0.0
WASHINGTON						
University of Washington Seattle, WA 98195 (206) 543-2212	51.4	45.9	37.5	72.2	31.0	25.0
Washington State University Pullman, WA 99164 (509) 335-0200	43.2	53.1	54.5	50.0	61.9	66.7
WEST VIRGINIA						
Marshall University Huntington, WV 25715 (304) 696-5408	30.3	38.8	36.8	50.0	45.8	33.3
West Virginia University Morgantown, WV 26506 (304) 293-5621	49.8	48.1	38.0	71.8	28.9	40.0
WISCONSIN						
University of Wisconsin Madison, WI 53706 (608) 262-5068	59.8	56.5	54.7	62.1	66.7	0.0
WYOMING						
University of Wyoming Laramie, WY 82071 (307) 766-2292	34.6	43.8	45.3	40.0	40.9	16.7

NCAA, Division I

These schools, while not competing at the highest level in football, still have major sports programs. Most compete in football at the I-AA level, which includes a year-end national championship play-off. Some (marked with an ✗ in the football section of the graduation rate survey) either have no football teams or have played Division III football. In a recent rules change, these must be in a new Division I-AAA football classification by 1993. Division I teams must offer at least six varsity sports for men's or mixed teams and six for women's teams now, with that number increasing to seven in each by the 1994-95 school year (indoor and outdoor track can be counted as two sports). With a few exceptions, such as the Ivy League, athletic scholarships are available in most sports.

	PERCENTAGE GRADUATING BY 1989					
	'84 freshman	'84 freshman athletes	male athletes	female athletes	'84 football recruits	'84 men's basketball recruits
ALABAMA						
Alabama State University Montgomery, AL 36101 (205) 293-4440	D/R					
Samford University Birmingham, AL 35229 (205) 870-2966	NA	50.0	50.0	NA	NA	0.0
University of Alabama at Birmingham Birmingham, AL 35294 (205) 934-3402	26.6	20.7	12.5	30.8	✗	0.0
University of South Alabama Mobile, AL 36688 (205) 460-7121	D/R					
ARIZONA						
Northern Arizona University ⸢lagstaff, AZ 86011 ‚602) 523-5353	D/R					
ARKANSAS						
Arkansas State University State University, AR 72467 (501) 972-3880	21.2	13.2	12.9	14.3	9.5	33.0
University of Arkansas Little Rock, AR 72204 (501) 569-3306	40.5	42.9	42.9	NA	✗	33.3

PERCENTAGE GRADUATING BY 1989

	'84 freshman	'84 freshman athletes	male athletes	female athletes	'84 football recruits	'84 men's basketball recruits
CALIFORNIA						
California State University Northridge, CA 91330 (818) 885-3208	15.5	10.7	8.1	15.8	12.5	50.0
Loyola Marymount University Los Angeles, CA 90045 (213) 338-2765	63.0	46.2	44.4	50.0	✗	50.0
Pepperdine University Malibu, CA 90263 (213) 456-4242	D/R					
St. Mary's College Moraga, CA 94575 (415) 631-4383	60.0	66.6	71.4	50.0	✗	66.7
Santa Clara University Santa Clara, CA 95053 (408) 554-5344	76.8	77.1	71.4	81.5	✗	60.0
U.S. International University San Diego, CA 92131 (619) 693-4554	NA					
University of California Irvine, CA 92717 (714) 856-6979	53.8	53.8	44.8	65.2	✗	0.0
University of California Santa Barbara, CA 93106 (805) 893-3400	57.7	56.5	62.2	50.0	✗	40.0
University of San Diego San Diego, CA 92100 (619) 260-4803	57.0	56.5	66.7	45.5	✗	0.0
University of San Francisco San Francisco, CA 94117-1080 (415) 666-6891	57.8	75.0	80.0	66.7	✗	n/a
CONNECTICUT						
Central Connecticut State University New Britain, CT 06050 (203) 827-7347	35.4	50.8	40.0	61.3	✗	50.0
Fairfield University Fairfield, CT 06430-7524 (203) 254-4040	82.0	77.8	60.0	100.0	✗	0.0
University of Connecticut Storrs, CT 06269 (203) 486-3863	62.0	54.1	41.9	76.6	52.6	25.0

PERCENTAGE GRADUATING BY 1989

	'84 freshman	'84 freshman athletes	male athletes	female athletes	'84 football recruits	'84 men's basketball recruits
University of Hartford West Hartford, CT 06117-1599 (203) 243-4989	44.0	90.9	85.7	94.7	✗	100.0
Yale University New Haven, CT 06520 (203) 432-1414	92.3	93.7	92.8	95.8	89.2	87.5
DELAWARE						
Delaware State College Dover, DE 19901 (302) 736-4928	D/R					
University of Delaware Newark, DE 19716 (302) 451-1818	66.2	71.7	66.7	84.8	56.4	57.1
DISTRICT OF COLUMBIA						
American University Washington, DC 20016-8061 (202) 885-3000	66.7	69.6	61.9	83.3	✗	80.0
George Washington University Washington, DC 20052 (202) 994-6650	63.3	78.0	84.2	72.7	✗	100.0
Georgetown University Washington, DC 20057 (202) 687-2435	83.9	90.6	91.7	87.5	✗	50.0
Howard University Washington, DC 20059 (202) 806-7140	D/R					
FLORIDA						
Bethune-Cookman College Daytona Beach, FL 32115 (904) 255-1401	D/R					
Florida A&M University Tallahassee, FL 32307 (904) 599-3868	25.9	20.5	17.9	27.8	18.2	14.3
Florida International University Miami, FL 33199 (305) 348-2761	37.1	40.9	28.6	62.5	✗	100.0
Jacksonville University Jacksonville, FL 32211 (904) 744-3950	44.5	44.4	38.9	55.6	✗	33.3

	'84 freshman	'84 freshman athletes	male athletes	female athletes	'84 football recruits	'84 men's basketball recruits
Stetson University DeLand, FL 32720 (904) 822-8100	58.9	56.1	55.6	57.12	✗	0.0
University of Central Florida Orlando, FL 32816 (407) 275-2994	34.1	42.3	30.8	53.8	✗	33.3
University of South Florida Tampa, FL 33620 (813) 974-2125	25.8	48.1	42.9	58.8	✗	0.0
GEORGIA						
Augusta College Augusta, GA 30910 (404) 737-1626	16.4	34.1	25.0	47.1	✗	0.0
Georgia Southern University Statesboro, GA 30460-8033 (912) 681-5376	30.5	50.0	57.1	0.0	57.1	0.0
Georgia State University Atlanta, GA 30303 (404) 651-2772	21.2	28.0	15.4	41.7	✗	0.0
Mercer University Macon, GA 31207 (912) 752-2994	31.4	50.0	45.5	100.0	✗	0.0
IDAHO						
Boise State University Boise, ID 83725 (208) 385-1981	21.2	21.7	10.0	43.8	25.0	0.0
Idaho State University Pocatello, ID 83201 (208) 236-2771	21.5	41.3	32.3	60.0	33.3	0.0
University of Idaho Moscow, ID 83843 (208) 885-0200	31.3	31.9	28.8	41.2	33.3	0.0
ILLINOIS						
Bradley University Peoria, IL 61625 (309) 677-2671	61.4	61.1	63.6	57.1	✗	57.1
Chicago State University Chicago, IL 60628 (312) 995-3661	8.1	24.4	20.6	42.9	✗	12.5

73

PERCENTAGE GRADUATING BY 1989

	'84 freshman	'84 freshman athletes	male athletes	female athletes	'84 football recruits	'84 men's basketball recruits
DePaul University Chicago, IL 60604-2287 (312) 362-8413	D/R					
Eastern Illinois University Charleston, IL 61920-3099 (217) 581-2106	46.9	54.0	49.0	71.4	35.7	75.0
Illinois State University Normal, IL 61761 (309) 438-3636	44.8	50.5	45.5	57.9	50.0	66.7
Loyola University Chicago, IL 60611 (312) 508-2560	58.8	73.3	63.6	100.0	✗	100.0
Northeastern Illinois University Chicago, IL 60625 (312) 794-3081	12.7	15.6	17.2	0.0	7.7	0.0
Southern Illinois University Carbondale, IL 62901 (618) 453-7250	39.5	37.2	22.4	56.8	16.7	100.0
University of Illinois, Chicago Chicago, IL 60680 (312) 996-2695	26.1	32.6	34.5	29.4	✗	0.0
Western Illinois University Macomb, IL 61455 (309) 298-1106	39.2	52.7	48.4	58.3	60.0	50.0

INDIANA

	'84 freshman	'84 freshman athletes	male athletes	female athletes	'84 football recruits	'84 men's basketball recruits
Butler University Indianapolis, IN 46208 (317) 283-9375	58.8	72.2	74.3	68.4	✗	0.0
University of Evansville Evansville, IN 47722 (812) 479-2238	D/R					
Indiana State University Terre Haute, IN 47809 (812) 237-4040	31.9	42.0	38.3	50.0	55.0	0.0
Valparaiso University Valparaiso, IN 46383 (219) 464-5230	70.6	60.3	57.4	66.7	✗	28.6

IOWA

	'84 freshman	'84 freshman athletes	male athletes	female athletes	'84 football recruits	'84 men's basketball recruits
Drake University Des Moines, IA 50311 (515) 271-2889	52.1	56.5	55.6	57.9	✗	100.0

PERCENTAGE GRADUATING BY 1989

	'84 freshman	'84 freshman athletes	male athletes	female athletes	'84 football recruits	'84 men's basketball recruits
University of Northern Iowa Cedar Falls, IA 50614 (319) 273-2470	44.0	50.0	46.7	57.9	50.0	50.0
KANSAS						
Wichita State University Wichita, KS 67208 (316) 689-3250	6.5	25.0	21.2	30.4	18.2	0.0
KENTUCKY						
Eastern Kentucky University Richmond, KY 40475-3101 (606) 622-3654	30.4	36.6	32.8	42.2	35.0	20.0
Morehead State University Morehead, KY 40351 (606) 783-2386	33.2	40.0	35.6	83.3	24.4	42.9
Murray State University Murray, KY 42071 (502) 762-6184	39.1	52.8	53.3	50.0	52.2	33.3
Western Kentucky University Bowling Green, KY 42101 (502) 745-3542	30.7	35.1	33.3	41.7	38.5	20.0
LOUISIANA						
Centenary College Shreveport, LA 71134 (318) 869-5275	35.9	53.7	50.0	71.4	✗	100.0
Grambling State University Grambling, LA 71245 (318) 274-2481	D/R					
McNeese State University Lake Charles, LA 70609 (318) 475-5215	17.6	15.3	15.6	14.3	23.8	0.0
Nicholls State University Thibodaux, LA 70310 (504) 448-4806	45.2	56.7	54.4	70.0	42.1	100.0
Northeast Louisiana University Monroe, LA 71209-3000 (318) 342-5361	21.1	24.0	22.4	29.4	40.9	0.0
Northwestern State University Natchitoches, LA 71497 (318) 357-5251	43.0	19.3	14.9	40.0	23.1	0.0

	'84 freshman	'84 freshman athletes	male athletes	female athletes	'84 football recruits	'84 men's basketball recruits
Southeastern Louisiana University Hammond, LA 70402 (504) 549-2253	22.9	23.6	20.0	40.0	3.7	0.0
Southern University Baton Rouge, LA 70813 (504) 771-3170	14.4	12.1	15.2	0.0	10.5	0.0
University of New Orleans New Orleans, LA 70148 (504) 286-7020	10.5	31.8	28.6	50.0	✘	25.0
MAINE						
University of Maine Orono, ME 04469 (207) 581-1057	49.5	56.8	53.1	70.6	56.3	66.7
MARYLAND						
Coppin State College Baltimore, MD 21216 (301) 333-5488	11.0	NA	NA	NA	NA	NA
Loyola College Baltimore, MD 21210 (301) 323-1010	57.5	56.0	50.0	63.6	✘	0.0
Morgan State University Baltimore, Md 21239 (301) 444-3050	D/R					
Mount St. Mary's College Emmitsburg, MD 21727 (301) 447-5296	70.6	80.0	90.0	66.7	✘	66.7
Towson State University Towson, MD 21204 (301) 830-2759	45.5	67.7	60.5	79.2	71.4	50.0
Univ. of MD, Baltimore County Baltimore, MD 21228 (301) 455-2207	29.3	48.5	42.1	57.1	✘	20.0
Univ. of MD, Eastern Shore Princess Anne, MD 21853 (301) 651-2200	43.2	28.6	17.9	42.9	✘	10.0
MASSACHUSETTS						
Boston University Boston, MA 02215 (617) 353-4630	D/R					

PERCENTAGE GRADUATING BY 1989

	'84 freshman	'84 freshman athletes	male athletes	female athletes	'84 football recruits	'84 men's basketball recruits
College of the Holy Cross Worcester, MA 01610-2395 (508) 793-2582	89.1	96.0	96.6	95.1	88.2	100.0
Harvard University Cambridge, MA 02138 (617) 495-2204	93.3	96.4	96.5	96.3	94.3	100.0
Northeastern University Boston, MA 02115 (617) 437-2672	D/R					
University of Massachusetts Amherst, MA 01003 (413) 545-2460	57.9	65.2	60.0	72.3	80.0	0.0
MICHIGAN						
University of Detroit Detroit, MI 48221 (313) 927-1720	D/R					
MISSISSIPPI						
Alcorn State University Lorman, MS 39096 (601) 877-3762	35.3	31.0	27.0	60.0	23.8	33.3
Jackson State University Jackson, MS 39217 (601) 968-2291	D/R					
Mississippi Valley State University Itta Bena, MS 38941 (601) 254-6641	23.1	64.7	65.3	63.2	64.0	75.0
MISSOURI						
St. Louis University St. Louis, MO 63108 (314) 658-3187	59.0	85.7	68.2	97.1	✗	50.0
Southwest MO State University Springfield, MO 65804 (417) 836-5244	30.5	51.0	46.6	63.0	58.8	33.3
University of Missouri Kansas City, MO 64110 (816) 235-1048	10.5	NA	NA	NA	NA	NA
MONTANA						
Montana State University Bozeman, MT 59717 (406) 994-4226	41.0	35.5	31.0	45.0	40.9	25.0

PERCENTAGE GRADUATING BY 1989

	'84 freshman	'84 freshman athletes	male athletes	female athletes	'84 football recruits	'84 men's basketball recruits
University of Montana Missoula, MT 59812 (406) 243-5331	29.0	24.6	20.0	32.0	13.6	25.0
NEBRASKA						
Creighton University Omaha, NE 68178-0001 (402) 280-2720	63.2	53.6	40.0	87.5	✗	25.0
NEVADA						
University of Nevada Reno, NV 89557 (702) 784-6900	37.5	46.5	43.3	53.8	66.7	100.0
NEW HAMPSHIRE						
Dartmouth College Hanover, NH 03755 (603) 646-2465	93.9	95.9	95.2	97.6	97.9	83.3
University of New Hampshire Durham, NH 03824 (603) 682-1850	62.1	74.4	69.8	81.8	59.3	33.3
NEW JERSEY						
Fairleigh Dickinson University Teaneck, NJ 07666 (201) 692-3980	D/R					
Monmouth College West Long Branch, NJ 07764 (201) 571-4295	46.9	60.8	63.4	50.0	✗	100.0
Princeton University Princeton, NJ 08544-0015 (609) 258-3535	93.3	97.4	96.6	100.0	96.6	100.0
Rider College Lawrenceville, NJ 08648-3099 (609) 896-5054	57.9	72.1	64.3	89.5	✗	66.7
St. Peter's College Jersey City, NJ 07306 (201) 915-9098	W/held	59.5	48.1	80.0	✗	33.3
Seton Hall University South Orange, NJ 07079 (201) 761-9497	55.4	50.0	44.4	57.1	✗	60.0

PERCENTAGE GRADUATING BY 1989

	'84 freshman	'84 freshman athletes	male athletes	female athletes	'84 football recruits	'84 men's basketball recruits
NEW YORK						
Brooklyn College Brooklyn, NY 11210 (718) 780-5366	D/R					
Canisius College Buffalo, NY 14208-1098 (716) 888-2970	56.0	58.1	57.1	60.0	✗	100.0
Colgate University Hamilton, NY 13346 (315) 824-1000	86.2	90.4	87.8	96.4	82.9	66.7
Columbia U./Barnard College New York, NY 10027 (212) 854-2537	85.4	87.1	84.3	96.3	73.2	100.0
Cornell University Ithaca, NY 14850 (607) 255-7265	84.6	82.7	80.9	86.9	80.3	100.0
Fordham University Bronx, NY 10458 (212) 579-2447	83.7	89.2	85.1	100.0	✗	33.3
Hofstra University Hempstead, NY 11550 (516) 560-6749	52.8	69.1	62.1	76.9	✗	100.0
Iona College New Rochelle, NY 10801 (914) 633-2311	64.9	61.1	56.8	80.0	✗	66.7
Long Island U./Brooklyn Center Brooklyn NY 11201 (718) 403-1030	D/R					
Manhattan College Riverdale, NY 10471 (212) 920-0230	69.8	80.0	66.7	88.9	✗	0.0
Marist College Poughkeepsie, NY 12601-1387 (914) 575-3699	60.0	69.8	66.7	76.5	✗	57.1
Niagara University Niagara University, NY 14109 (716) 285-1212	59.8	69.6	53.8	90.0	✗	50.0
St. Bonaventure University St. Bonaventure, NY 14778 (716) 375-2210	68.4	85.0	80.6	100.0	✗	100.0
St. Francis College Brooklyn Heights, NY 11201 (718) 522-2300	20.1	69.7	63.6	81.8	✗	0.0

	'84 freshman	'84 freshman athletes	male athletes	female athletes	'84 football recruits	'84 men's basketball recruits
St. John's University Jamaica, NY 11439 (718) 990-6224	63.1	78.4	76.5	82.4	✗	100.0
Siena College Loudonville, NY 12211-1462 (518) 783-2531	74.8	90.1	85.7	100.0	✗	66.7
Wagner College Staten Island, NY 10301 (718) 390-3433	26.7	42.1	46.2	33.3	✗	50.0
NORTH CAROLINA						
Appalachian State University Boone, NC 28608 (704) 262-4010	50.0	42.7	38.2	64.3	35.1	33.0
Campbell University Buies Creek, NC 27506 (919) 893-4111	D/R					
Davidson College Davidson, NC 28036 (704) 892-2373	88.6	86.8	83.9	100.0	75.0	66.7
North Carolina A&T State Univ. Greensboro, NC 27411 (919) 334-7686	32.0	12.5	12.8	0.0	7.7	16.7
University of North Carolina Asheville, NC 28804 (704) 251-6459	27.1	38.9	33.3	44.4	✗	50.0
University of North Carolina Charlotte, NC 28223 (704) 547-4920	D/R					
University of North Carolina Wilmington, NC 28403-3297 (919) 395-3230	38.0	67.3	82.6	53.8	✗	50.0
Western Carolina University Cullowhee, NC 28723 (704) 227-7338	36.9	36.0	31.8	66.7	35.7	0.0
OHIO						
Cleveland State University Cleveland, OH 44115 (216) 687-4808	14.8	23.1	17.9	36.4	✗	0.0
University of Dayton Dayton, OH 45469 (513) 229-2111	67.4	76.9	88.9	50.0	✗	100.0

80

	PERCENTAGE GRADUATING BY 1989					
	'84 freshman	'84 freshman athletes	male athletes	female athletes	'84 football recruits	'84 men's basketball recruits
Wright State University Dayton, OH 45435-0001 (513) 873-2771	25.1	42.4	50.0	27.3	✗	33.3
Xavier University Cincinnati, OH 45207 (513) 745-3413	60.3	79.1	77.8	81.3	✗	100.0
Youngstown State University Youngstown, OH 44555-0001 (216) 742-3718	24.8	41.5	28.9	73.3	33.3	33.3
OREGON						
University of Portland Portland, OR 97203-5798 (503) 283-7117	49.4	62.0	64.5	57.9	✗	0.0
PENNSYLVANIA						
Bucknell University Lewisburg, PA 17837 (717) 524-3301	87.3	86.9	86.8	87.1	88.6	100.0
Drexel University Philadelphia, PA 19104 (215) 590-8930	63.9	91.9	91.3	93.8	✗	60.0
Duquesne University Pittsburgh, PA 15282 (412) 434-6565	69.7	92.2	90.9	100.0	✗	66.7
LaSalle University Philadelphia, PA 19141-1199 (215) 951-1516	71.4	71.8	66.7	78.8	✗	80.0
Lafayette College Easton, PA 18042 (215) 250-5470	86.7	83.6	82.5	87.5	72.7	100.0
Lehigh University Bethlehem, PA 18015 (215) 758-4320	83.8	84.7	81.7	91.1	70.6	70.0
Robert Morris College Coraopolis, PA 15108-1189 (412) 262-8302	51.6	69.2	59.3	91.7	✗	20.0
St. Francis College Loretto, PA 15940-9989 (814) 472-3276	57.4	63.6	50.0	71.4	✗	50.0
St. Joseph's University Philadelphia, PA 19131 (215) 660-1707	71.2	83.3	73.7	100.0	✗	50.0

PERCENTAGE GRADUATING BY 1989

	'84 freshman	'84 freshman athletes	male athletes	female athletes	'84 football recruits	'84 men's basketball recruits
University of Pennsylvania Philadelphia, PA 19104 (215) 898-6121	87.7	83.2	79.1	93.0	76.1	66.7
Villanova University Villanova, PA 19085 (215) 645-4111	83.6	87.5	83.7	91.5	✘	50.0
RHODE ISLAND						
Brown University Providence, RI 02912 (401) 863-2343	89.9	89.2	88.3	91.4	88.1	85.7
Providence College Providence, RI 02918 (401) 865-2265	D/R					
University of Rhode Island Kingston, RI 02881 (401) 792-5245	49.3	58.9	60.5	56.7	76.9	33.3
SOUTH CAROLINA						
Baptist College Charleston, SC 29411 (803) 797-4116	D/R					
The Citadel Charleston, SC 29409 (803) 792-5030	66.9	83.3	83.3	none enrolled	85.7	50.0
Coastal Carolina College Conway, SC 29256 (803) 347-3161	22.3	33.3	26.9	50.0	✘	28.6
Furman University Greenville, SC 29613 (803) 294-2150	75.8	76.9	83.1	56.0	84.2	100.0
South Carolina State College Orangeburg, SC 29117 (803) 536-7242	48.3	33.8	29.1	60.0	29.6	66.7
Winthrop College Rock Hill, SC 29733 (803) 329-2140	40.3	35.1	34.8	35.7	*	20.0
TENNESSEE						
Austin Peay State University Clarksville, TN 37044-4576 (615) 648-7903	23.4	25.9	20.9	45.5	13.0	16.7

82

PERCENTAGE GRADUATING BY 1989

	'84 freshman	'84 freshman athletes	male athletes	female athletes	'84 football recruits	'84 men's basketball recruits
East Tennessee State University Johnson City, TN 37614 (615) 929-4343	24.0	42.1	37.0	54.5	41.2	50.0
Middle Tennessee State University Murfreesboro, TN 37132 (615) 898-2450	25.5	20.0	14.3	42.9	21.1	0.0
Tennessee State University Nashville, TN 37209-1561 (615) 320-3598	7.5	28.2	23.3	44.4	28.6	0.0
Tennessee Technological University Cookeville, TN 38505-0001 (615) 372-3949	28.1	43.8	41.6	50.0	0.0	100.0
Univ. of TN at Chattanooga Chattanooga, TN 37403-2598 (615) 755-4495	23.0	16.9	10.0	40.0	15.4	0.0

TEXAS

	'84 freshman	'84 freshman athletes	male athletes	female athletes	'84 football recruits	'84 men's basketball recruits
Hardin-Simmons University Abilene, TX 79698 (915) 670-1435	42.2	60.0	60.0	60.0	✗	100.0
Lamar University Beaumont, TX 77710 (409) 880-8323	14.6	10.5	8.8	21.4	7.0	0.0
Prairie View A&M University Prairie View, TX 77446 (409) 857-2224	65.0	63.4	60.0	83.3	25.0	100.0
Sam Houston State University Huntsville, TX 77341 (409) 294-1160	28.1	34.0	32.4	38.5	25.0	0.0
Southwest Texas State University San Marcos, TX 78666-4615 (512) 245-2114	44.0	41.2	40.6	42.9	42.5	66.7
Stephen F. Austin State University Nacogdoches, TX 75962 (409) 568-3501	35.3	29.5	23.4	50.0	19.2	50.0
Texas Southern University Houston, TX 77004 (713) 527-7271	44.6	9.4	8.2	13.3	0.0	100.0
University of North Texas Denton, TX 76203-3737 (817) 565-2451	24.3	17.9	11.5	40.0	7.1	0.0
Univ. of Texas at Arlington Arlington, TX 76019 (817) 273-2261	15.3	16.7	18.2	15.4	✗	50.0

PERCENTAGE GRADUATING BY 1989

	'84 freshman	'84 freshman athletes	male athletes	female athletes	'84 football recruits	'84 men's basketball recruits
Univ. of Texas, Pan American Edinburg, TX 78539-2999 (512) 381-2221	10.7	10.0	10.0	n/a	✘	33.3
Univ. of Texas at San Antonio San Antonio, TX 78285 (512) 691-4444	10.2	16.7	50.0	0.0	✘	75.0
UTAH						
Southern Utah State College Cedar City, UT 84720 (801) 586-7857	NA	NA	NA	NA	NA	NA
Weber State College Ogden, UT 84408 (801) 626-6817	11.1	32.8	31.1	36.8	35.0	0.0
VERMONT						
University of Vermont Burlington, VT 05405 (802) 656-3074	72.5	85.2	80.9	91.2	✘	100.0
VIRGINIA						
George Mason University Fairfax, VA 22030 (703) 323-3462	33.6	51.7	45.7	60.9	✘	40.0
James Madison University Harrisonburg, VA 22807 (703) 568-6164	74.3	72.0	69.6	76.5	51.6	50.0
Liberty University Lynchburg, VA 24502 (804) 582-2100	D/R					
Old Dominion University Norfolk, VA 23529 (804) 683-3369	45.3	49.3	46.0	58.8	✘	66.7
Radford University Radford, VA 24142 (703) 831-5228	48.5	63.5	60.5	68.0	✘	50.0
University of Richmond Richmond, VA 23173-1903 (804) 289-8370	80.4	80.4	75.7	92.9	66.7	100.0
Virginia Commonwealth University Richmond, VA 23284-2512 (804) 367-1280	37.5	44.2	41.7	47.4	✘	0.0

PERCENTAGE GRADUATING BY 1989

	'84 freshman	'84 freshman athletes	male athletes	female athletes	'84 football recruits	'84 men's basketball recruits
Virginia Military Institute Lexington, VA 24450 (703) 464-7251	64.3	64.8	64.8	none enrolled	69.7	25.0
College of William and Mary Williamsburg, VA 23187 (804) 221-3330	84.1	84.7	80.4	91.2	85.0	50.0
WASHINGTON						
Eastern Washington University Cheney, WA 99004 (509) 359-2463	27.2	27.7	22.0	46.7	21.7	0.0
Gonzaga University Spokane, WA 99258 (509) 328-4220	48.8	100.0	100.0	100.0	✗	100.0
WISCONSIN						
Marquette University Milwaukee, WI 53233 (414) 288-6303	71.6	87.5	85.7	90.0	✗	33.3
Univ. of Wisconsin, Green Bay Green Bay, WI 54311-7001 (414) 465-2145	25.9	42.9	54.5	30.0	✗	33.3
Univ. of Wisconsin, Milwaukee Milwaukee, WI 53201 (414) 229-5669	NA	NA	NA	NA	NA	NA

NCAA, Division II

Just a step behind Division I in the size of athletic programs, these schools can be just as competitive in seeking out athletes. Division II schools must offer four varsity sports for men's or mixed teams and four for women's. There are play-offs in all sports, including football, and scholarships are offered in most sports.

ALABAMA

Alabama A&M University	Normal, AL 35762	(205) 851-5360	Div. I in men's soccer
Jacksonville State University	Jacksonville, AL 36265	(205) 782-5365	
Livingston University	Livingston, AL 35470	(205) 652-9661	
Miles College	Birmingham, AL 35208	(205) 923-2771	
Troy State Univrsity	Troy, AL 36082	(205) 566-8112	
Tuskegee University	Tuskegee, AL 36088	(205) 727-8849	
University of Alabama	Huntsville, AL 35899	(205) 895-6144	
University of North Alabama	Florence, AL 35632	(205) 760-4397	

ALASKA

University of Alaska	Anchorage, AK 99508	(907) 786-1230	
University of Alaska	Fairbanks, AK 99775-0500	(907) 474-7205	

ARIZONA

Grand Canyon University	Phoenix, AZ 85017	(602) 589-2806	Div. I in baseball

CALIFORNIA

California Lutheran University	Thousand Oaks, CA 91360-2787	(805) 493-3402	
CA Polytechnic State Univ.	San Luis Obispo, CA 93407	(805) 756-2923	Div. I in wrestling, women's volleyball
CA Polytechnic State Univ.	Pomona, CA 91768	(714) 869-2811	Div. I in softball
California State University	Bakersfield, CA 93311-1099	(805) 664-2200	Div. I in wrestling
California State University	Chico, CA 95929-0300	(916) 898-6470	
CA State Univ., Dominguez Hills	Carson, CA 90747	(213) 516-3893	
California State University	Hayward, CA 94542	(415) 881-3038	
California State University	Los Angeles, CA 90032-8240	(213) 343-3080	Div. I in men's soccer
California State University	Sacramento, CA 95819	(916) 278-6348	Div. I in baseball, softball
CA State U., Stanislaus	Turlock, CA 95380	(209) 667-3566	
Chapman College	Orange, CA 92666	(714) 997-6691	
Humboldt State University	Arcata, CA 95521	(707) 826-3666	
Notre Dame, College of	Belmont, CA 94002	(415) 593-1601	
San Francisco State University	San Francisco, CA 94132	(415) 338-2218	
Sonoma State University	Rohnert Park, CA 94928	(707) 664-2521	
University of California	Davis, CA 95616	(916) 752-9363	
University of California	Riverside, CA 92521	(714) 787-5432	

COLORADO

Adams State College	Alamosa, CO 81102	(719) 589-7401	
Colorado Christian University	Lakewood, CO 80226	(303) 238-5386	
Colorado School of Mines	Golden, CO 80401	(303) 273-3368	
Fort Lewis College	Durango, CO 81301-3999	(303) 247-7571	

Mesa State College	Grand Junction, CO 81501	(303) 248-1503	
Metropolitan State Coll. of Denver	Denver, CO 80217-3362	(303) 556-8300	
Regis College	Denver, CO 80221	(303) 458-4070	
University of Colorado	Colorado Springs, CO 80933-7150	(719) 593-3575	
University of Denver	Denver, CO 80208	(303) 871-3399	Div. I in ice hockey, women's gymnastics
University of Northern Colorado	Greeley, CO 80639	(303) 351-2534	
University of Southern Colorado	Pueblo, CO 81001-4901	(719) 549-2711	
Western State College of Colorado	Gunnison, CO 81231	(303) 943-2079	

CONNECTICUT

Quinnipiac College	Hamden, CT 06518	(203) 281-8621	
Sacred Heart University	Fairfield, CT 06432-1000	(203) 371-7827	
Southern Connecticut State Univ.	New Haven, CT 06515	(203) 397-4378	Div. I in men's gymnastics
University of Bridgeport	Bridgeport, CT 06601	(203) 576-4735	
University of New Haven	West Haven, CT 06516	(203) 932-7016	

DISTRICT OF COLUMBIA

U. of the District of Columbia	Washington, DC 20008	(202) 282-7748

FLORIDA

Barry University	Miami Shores, FL 33161	(305) 758-3392	
Eckerd College	St. Petersburg, FL 33733	(813) 867-1166	
Florida Atlantic University	Boca Raton, FL 33431-0991	(407) 367-3710	
FL Institute of Technology	Melbourne, FL 32901	(407) 768-8000	
Florida Southern College	Lakeland, FL 33801-5698	(813) 680-4254	
Rollins College	Winter Park, FL 32789	(407) 646-2198	Div. I in women's tennis
St. Leo College	St. Leo, FL 33574	(904) 588-8221	
University of Tampa	Tampa, FL 33606-1940	(813) 253-6240	

GEORGIA

Albany State College	Albahy, GA 31705	(912) 430-4754
Armstrong State College	Savannah, GA 31419-1997	(912) 927-5336
Clark Atlanta University	Atlanta, GA 30314	(404) 880-8123
Columbus College	Columbus, GA 31993-2399	(404) 568-2204
Fort Valley State College	Fort Valley, GA 31030	(912) 825-6208
Georgia College	Milledgeville, GA 31061	(912) 453-4072
Morehouse College	Atlanta, GA 30314	(404) 681-2800
Morris Brown College	Atlanta, GA 30314	(404) 525-7831
Paine College	Augusta, GA 30910	(404) 722-4471
Savannah State College	Savannah, GA 31404	(912) 356-2228
Valdosta College	Valdosta, GA 31698	(912) 333-5890
West Georgia College	Carrollton, GA 30118	(404) 836-6533

HAWAII

Chaminade University	Honolulu, HI 96816	(808) 735-4790

ILLINOIS

Lewis University	Romeoville, IL 60441	(815) 838-0500	
Quincy College	Quincy, IL 62301-2699	(217) 228-5290	Div. I in men's soccer
Southern Illinois University	Edwardsville, IL 62026	(618) 692-2871	Div. I in men's soccer

87

INDIANA

Indiana Univ./Purdue Univ.	Fort Wayne, IN 46805	(219) 481-6643
Oakland City College	Oakland City, IN 47660	(812) 749-1290
St. Joseph's College	Rensselaer, IN 47978	(219) 866-6338
University of Indianapolis	Indianapolis, IN 46227	(317) 788-3248
University of Southern Indiana	Evansville, IN 47712	(812) 464-1846

IOWA

Morningside College	Sioux City, IA 51106	(712) 274-5312

KANSAS

Emporia State University	Emporia, KS 66801-5087	(316) 343-5354
Fort Hays State University	Hays, KS 67601	(913) 628-4050
Pittsburg State University	Pittsburg, KS 66762	(316) 235-4653
Washburn Univ. of Topeka	Topeka, KS 66621	(913) 295-6334

KENTUCKY

Bellarmine College	Louisville, KY 40205	(502) 452-8381
Kentucky State University	Frankfort, KY 40601	(502) 227-6011
Kentucky Wesleyan University	Owensboro, KY 43202-1039	(502) 926-3111
Northern Kentucky University	Highland Heights, Ky 41706-1448	(606) 572-5631

MARYLAND

Bowie State University	Bowie, MD 20715	(301) 464-6514

MASSACHUSETTS

American International College	Springfield, MA 01109	(413) 737-7000	
Assumption College	Worcester, MA 01615-0005	(508) 752-5615	
Bentley College	Waltham, MA 02154-4705	(617) 891-2330	
Merrimack College	North Andover, MA 01845	(508) 683-7113	Div. I in ice hockey
Springfield College	Springfield, MA 01109	(413) 788-3484	Div. I in field hockey
Stonehill College	North Easton, MA 02357	(508) 230-1384	
University of Lowell	Lowell, MA 01854	(508) 934-2310	Div. I in ice hockey

MICHIGAN

Ferris State University	Big Rapids, MI 49307-2295	(616) 592-2860	Div. I in ice hockey
Grand Valley State University	Allendale, MI 49401	(616) 895-3259	
Hillsdale College	Hillsdale, MI 49242	(517) 437-7364	
Lake Superior State University	Sault Ste. Marie, MI 49783	(906) 635-2366	Div. I in ice hockey
Michigan Technological University	Houghton, MI 49931-1295	(906) 487-2715	Div. I in ice hockey
Northern Michigan University	Marquette, MI49855	(906) 227-1211	Div. I in ice hockey
Oakland University	Rochester, MI 48309-4401	(313) 370-3196	
Saginaw Valley State University	University Center, MI 48710	(517) 791-7300	
Wayne State University	Detroit, MI 48202	(313) 577-4280	

MINNESOTA

Bemidji State University	Bemidji, MN 56601-2699	(218) 755-2767	
Mankato State University	Mankato, MN 56002-8400	(507) 389-1795	
St. Cloud State University	St. Cloud, MN 56301-4498	(612) 255-3102	
University of Minnesota	Duluth, MN 55812	(218) 726-8168	Div. I in ice hockey
Winona State University	Winona, MN 55987	(507) 457-5212	

MISSISSIPPI

Delta State University	Cleveland, MS 38733	(601) 846-4300
Mississippi College	Clinton, MS 39058	(601) 925-3342
Mississippi University for Women	Columbus, MS 39701	(601) 329-7225

MISSOURI

Central Missouri State University	Warrensburg, MO 64093	(816) 429-4521
Lincoln University	Jefferson City, MO 65101	(314) 681-5327
Missouri Southern State College	Joplin, MO 64801	(417) 625-9317
Missouri Western State College	St. Joseph, MO 64507	(816) 271-4482
Northeast Missouri State University	Kirksville, MO 63501	(816) 785-4236
Northwest Missouri State University	Maryville, MO 64468-6001	(816) 562-1306
Southeast Missouri State University	Cape Girardeau, MO 63701	(314) 651-2229
Southwest Baptist University	Bolivar, MO 65613	(417) 326-1747
University of Missouri	Rolla, MO 65401	(314) 341-4177
University of Missouri	St. Louis, MO 63121	(314) 553-5641

MONTANA

Eastern Montana College	Billings, MT 59101	(406) 657-2369

NEBRASKA

Chadron State College	Chadron, NE 69337	(308) 432-6345
Kearney State College	Kearney, NE 68849	(308) 234-8514
University of Nebraska	Omaha, NE 68182	(402) 554-2533
Wayne State College	Wayne, NE 68787	(402) 375-2200

NEW HAMPSHIRE

Franklin Pierce College	Rindge, NH 03641	(603) 899-4100
Keene State College	Keene, NH 03431-4183	(603) 352-1909
New Hampshire College	Manchester, NH 03104	(603) 668-2211
St. Anselm College	Manchester, NH 03102	(603) 641-7800

NEW MEXICO

Eastern New Mexico University	Portales, NM 88130	(505) 562-2153

NEW YORK

Adelphi University	Garden City, NY 11530	(516) 663-1155	Div. I in men's soccer, softball
Buffalo, State Univ. of New York	Buffalo, NY 14260	(716) 636-3456	
Concordia College	Bronxville, NY 10708	(914) 337-9300	
Dowling College	Oakdale, NY 11769-1999	(516) 244-3342	
LeMoyne College	Syracuse, NY 13214	(315) 445-4412	Div. I in baseball
Long Island Univ./C.W. Post Campus	Brookville, NY 11548	(516) 299-2289	Div. I in baseball
Mercy College	Dobbs Ferry, NY 10522	(914) 693-4500	
Molloy College	Rockville Centre, NY 11570	(516) 678-5000	
New York Institute of Technology	Old Westbury, NY 11568	(516) 686-7626	Div. I in baseball
Pace University	Pleasantville, NY 10570-2799	(914) 773-3411	Div. I in baseball
Queens College	Flushing, NY 11367	(718) 520-7215	
St. Rose, College of	Albany, NY 12203	(518) 454-5282	
Southampton Campus of Long Island U.	Southampton, NY 11968	(516) 283-4000	

NORTH CAROLINA

Elizabeth City State University	Elizabeth City, N.C. 27909	(919) 335-3385
Fayetteville State University	Fayetteville, N.C. 28301	(919) 486-1314

Johnson C. Smith University	Charlotte, N.C. 28216	(704) 378-1072	
Lenoir-Rhyne College	Hickory, N.C. 28603	(704) 328-7115	
Livingstone College	Salisbury, N.C. 28144	(704) 638-5592	
North Carolina Central University	Durham, N.C. 27707	(919) 560-6574	
Pembroke State University	Pembroke, N.C. 28372	(919) 521-9481	
Pfeiffer College	Misenheimer, N.C. 28109	(704) 463-1360	
Queens College	Charlotte, N.C. 28274	(704) 337-2510	
St. Augustine's College	Raleigh, N.C. 27611	(919) 828-4451	
Shaw University	Raleigh, N.C. 27611	(919) 755-4978	
University of North Carolina	Greensboro, N.C. 27412	(919) 334-5213	
Winston-Salem State University	Winston-Salem, N.C. 27110	(919) 750-2592	

NORTH DAKOTA

North Dakota State University	Fargo, ND 58105	(701) 237-8985	
University of North Dakota	Grand Forks, ND 58202	(701) 777-2234	Div. I in ice hockey

OHIO

Ashland University.	Ashland, OH 44805	(419) 289-5400	

OKLAHOMA

Cameron University	Lawton, OK 73505	(405) 581-2300	
Central State University	Edmond, OK 73034	(405) 341-2980	

OREGON

Portland State University	Portland, OR 97207-0751	(503) 725-4000	Div. I in baseball, women's basketball

PENNSYLVANIA

Bloomsburg University of PA	Bloomsburg, PA 17815	(717) 389-4363	Div. I in wrestling, Div. III in field hockey
California University of PA	California, PA 15419	(412) 938-4351	
Cheyney University of PA	Cheyney, PA 19319	(215) 399-2287	
Clarion University of PA	Clarion, PA 16214	(814) 226-1997	Div. I in wrestling
East Stroudsburg University of PA	East Stroudsburg, PA 18301	(717) 424-3642	Div. I in wrestling, Div. III in field hockey
Edinboro University of PA	Edinboro, PA 16444-0001	(814) 732-2776	Div. I in wrestling
Gannon University	Erie, PA 16541	(814) 871-7415	
Indiana University of PA	Indiana, PA 15705	(412) 357-2751	Div. III in field hockey
Kutztown University of PA	Kutztown, PA 19530-0721	(215) 683-4095	Div. I in wrestling, Div. III in field hockey
Lock Haven University of PA	Lock Haven, PA 17745	(717) 893-2102	Div. I in wrestling, Div. III in field hockey
Mansfield University of PA	Mansfield, PA 16933	(717) 662-4636	Div. III in field hockey
Mercyhurst College	Erie, PA 16546	(814) 825-0226	
Millersville University of PA	Millersville, PA 17551	(717) 872-3361	Div. I in wrestling, Div. III in field hockey
Phil. Coll. of Textiles and Science	Philadelphia, PA 19144	(215) 951-2713	Div. I in men's soccer
Shippensburg University of PA	Shippensburg, PA 17257	(717) 532-1711	Div. I in wrestling
Slippery Rock University of PA	Slippery Rock, PA 16057	(412) 794-7336	Div. I in wrestling, Div. III in field hockey
University of Pittsburgh	Johnstown, PA 15904	(814) 269-2001	
West Chester University of PA	West Chester, PA 19383	(215) 436-3555	Div. I in baseball, field hockey

RHODE ISLAND
Bryant College	Smithfield, RI 02917-1284	(401) 232-6070

SOUTH CAROLINA
Erskine College	Due West, SC 29639	(803) 379-8701
Newberry College	Newberry, SC 29108	(803) 276-5010
University of South Carolina	Aiken, SC 29801	(803) 648-6851
University of South Carolina	Spartanburg, SC 29303	(803) 599-2141
Wofford College	Spartanburg, SC 29303-3840	(803) 585-4821

SOUTH DAKOTA
Augustana College	Sioux Falls, S.D. 57197	(605) 336-4315
South Dakota State University	Brookings, S.D. 57007	(605) 688-5625
University of South Dakota	Vermillion, S.D. 57069-2390	(605) 677-5951

TENNESSEE
LeMoyne-Owen College	Memphis, TN 38126	(901) 942-7359
Lincoln Memorial University	Harrogate, TN 37752	(615) 869-6238
University of Tennessee	Martin, TN 38238-5021	(901) 587-7671

TEXAS
Abilene Christian University	Abilene, TX 79699	(915) 674-2108
Angelo State University	San Angelo, TX 76909	(915) 942-2091
East Texas State University	Commerce, TX 75429-3011	(214) 886-5100
Houston Baptist University	Houston, TX 77074-3298	(713) 995-3314 Div. I in men's gymnastics
Texas A&I University	Kingsville, TX 78363	(512) 595-2499
Texas Woman's University	Denton, TX 76204	(817) 898-2378
West Texas State University	Canyon, TX 79016-0997	(806) 656-2680

VERMONT
St. Michael's College	Colchester, VT 05439	(802) 655-2000

VIRGINIA
Hampton University	Hampton, VA 23668	(804) 727-5641
Longwood College	Farmville, VA 23901	(804) 395-2058
Norfolk State University	Norfolk, VA 23504	(804) 683-8152
St. Paul's College	Lawrenceville, VA 23868	(804) 848-2001
Virginia State University	Petersburg, VA 23803-2096	(804) 524-5030
Virginia Union University	Richmond, VA 23220	(804) 257-5890

WASHINGTON
Seattle Pacific University	Seattle, WA 98119	(205) 281-2085

WEST VIRGINIA
Davis and Elkins College	Elkins, WV 26241	(304) 636-1900 Div. I in field hockey
Shepherd College	Shepherdstown, WV 25443	(304) 876-2511

WISCONSIN
University of Wisconsin	Parkside, WI 53141-2000	(414) 533-2308

NCAA, Division III

These smaller, often private schools, have no athletic scholarships. Financial aid is offered on the basis of need only, and student-athletes cannot be treated more favorably than other students. Still, many have very competitive sports programs. Division III schools must offer four varsity sports for men's or mixed teams and four for women's. There are play-offs in all sports.

ALABAMA

Stillman College	Tuscaloosa, AL 35403	(205) 349-4240

CALIFORNIA

California Institute of Technology	Pasadena, CA 91125	(818) 356-6146	
California State University	San Bernardino, CA 92407-2397	(714) 880-5011	
Claremont McKenna- H.Mudd-Scripps	Claremont, CA 91711	(714) 621-8000	
Menlo College	Atherton, CA 94205-4185	(415) 688-3772	
Mills College	Oakland, CA 94613	(415) 430-2172	
Occidental College	Los Angeles, CA 90041	(213) 259-2608	
Pomona-Pitzer Colleges	Claremont, CA 91711	(714) 621-8016	
Univ. of California, San Diego	La Jolla, CA 92093-0905	(619) 534-4211	
University of California	Santa Cruz, CA 95064	(408) 459-2531	
University of La Verne	La Verne, CA 91750	(714) 593-3511	
University of Redlands	Redlands, CA 92373-0999	(714) 793-2121	
Whittier College	Whittier, CA 90608	(213) 693-0771	

COLORADO

Colorado College	Colorado Springs, CO 80903	(719) 389-6493	Div. I in ice hockey, women's soccer

CONNECTICUT

Albertus Magnus College	New Haven, CT 06511	(203) 773-8550
Connecticut College	New London, CT 06320	(203) 447-1911
Eastern Connecticut State Univ.	Willimantic, CT 06226	(203) 456-5458
Trinity College	Hartford, CT 06106	(203) 297-2057
U.S. Coast Guard Academy	New London, CT 06320-4195	(203) 444-8600
Wesleyan University	Middletown, CT 06457	(203) 344-7907
Western Connecticut State Univ.	Danbury, CT 06810	(203) 797-4239

DELAWARE

Wesley College	Dover, DE 19901	(302) 736-2450

DISTRICT OF COLUMBIA

Catholic University	Washington, DC 20064	(202) 319-5286
Gallaudet University	Washington, DC 20002	(202) 651-5603

GEORGIA

Emory University	Atlanta, GA 30322	(404) 727-6547
Oglethorpe University	Atlanta, GA 30319	(404) 261-1441

ILLINOIS

Augustana College	Rock Island, IL 61201	(309) 794-7523
Aurora University	Aurora, IL 60506	(708) 844-5112
Blackburn College	Carlinville, IL 62626	(217) 854-7831
Concordia University	River Forest, IL 60305	(312) 771-8300
Elmhurst College	Elmhurst, IL 60126	(708) 617-3142
Eureka College	Eureka, IL 61530	(309) 467-6373
Illinois Benedictine College	Lisle, IL 60532-0900	(708) 960-1500
Illinois College	Jacksonville, IL 62650	(217) 245-3400
Illinois Wesleyan University	Bloomington, IL 61702-2900	(309) 556-3345
Knox College	Galesburg, IL 61401	(309) 343-0112
Lake Forest College	Lake Forest, IL 60045	(708) 234-3100
MacMurray College	Jacksonville, IL 62650	(217) 479-7142
Millikin University	Decatur, IL 62522-2084	(217) 424-6344
Monmouth College	Monmouth, IL 61462	(309) 457-2176
North Central College	Naperville, IL 60566	(708) 420-3472
North Park College	Chicago, IL 60625	(312) 583-2700
Parks College of St. Louis U.	Cahokia, IL 62206	(618) 337-7500
Principia College	Elsah, IL 62028	(618) 374-5025
Rockford College	Rockford, IL 61108	(815) 226-4085
University of Chicago	Chicago, IL 60637	(312) 702-7684
Wheaton College	Wheaton, IL 60187-5593	(708) 260-5125

INDIANA

DePauw University	Greencastle, IN 46135	(317) 658-4934
Earlham College	Richmond, IN 47374	(317) 983-1489
Rose-Hulman Inst. of Technology	Terre Haute, IN 47803	(812) 877-1511
Saint Mary's College	Notre Dame, IN 46556-5001	(219) 284-5548
Wabash College	Crawfordsville, IN 47933	(317) 364-4233

IOWA

Buena Vista College	Storm Lake, IA 50588-9990	(712) 749-2253
Central College	Pella, IA 50219	(515) 628-5224
Coe College	Cedar Rapids, IA 52402	(319) 399-8599
Cornell College	Mount Vernon, IA 52314	(319) 895-4267
Grinnell College	Grinnell, IA 50112	(515) 269-3800
Loras College	Dubuque, IA 52004-0178	(319) 588-7112
Luther College	Decorah, IA 52101	(319) 387-1583
Simpson College	Indianola, IA 50125	(515) 961-1620
University of Dubuque	Dubuque, IA 52001	(319) 589-3225
Upper Iowa University	Fayette, IA 52142	(319) 425-5291
Wartburg College	Waverly, IA 50677	(319) 352-8470
William Penn College	Oskaloosa, IA 52577	(515) 673-1020

KENTUCKY

Asbury College	Wilmore, KY 40390	(606) 858-3511
Berea College	Berea, KY 40404	(606) 986-9341
Centre College	Danville, KY 40422	(606) 236-5211
Thomas More College	Crestview Hills, KY 41017-3428	(606) 344-3536

MAINE

Bates College	Lewiston, ME 04240	(207) 786-6351
Bowdoin College	Brunswick, ME 04011	(207) 725-3666
Colby College	Waterville, ME 04901	(207) 872-3364
Gordon College	Wenham, ME 01984	(508) 927-2300
Maine Maritime Academy	Castine, ME 04421	(207) 326-4311

St. Joseph's College	North Windham, ME 04062	(207) 892-6766
Univ of Maine at Farmington	Farmington, ME 04938	(207) 778-3501
University of Southern Maine	Gorham, ME 04038	(207) 780-5431

MARYLAND

Frostburg State University	Frostburg, MD 21532-1099	(301) 689-4471	
Goucher College	Towson, MD 21204	(301) 337-6385	
Hood College	Frederick, MD 21701	(301) 663-3131	
Johns Hopkins University	Baltimore, MD 21218	(301) 338-7490	Div. I in men's lacrosse
Notre Dame, College of	Baltimore, MD 21210	(301) 532-5378	
St. Mary's College of Maryland	St. Mary's City, MD 20686	(301) 862-0318	
Salisbury State University	Salisbury, MD 21801	(301) 543-6340	
Washington College	Chestertown, MD 21620	(301) 778-2800	
Western Maryland College	Westminster, MD 21157	(301) 857-2571	

MASSACHUSETTS

Amherst College	Amherst, MA 01002	(413) 542-2274
Anna Maria College	Paxton, MA 01612	(508) 757-4586
Babson College	Wellesley, MA 02157	(617) 239-4594
Brandeis University	Waltham, MA 02254	(617) 736-3630
Bridgewater State College	Bridgewater, MA 02325-9998	(508) 697-1352
Clark University	Worcester, MA 01610	(508) 793-7160
Curry College	Milton, MA 02186	(617) 333-0500
Eastern Nazarene College	Quincy, MA 02170	(617) 773-6350
Emerson College	Boston, MA 02116	(617) 578-8690
Emmanuel College	Boston, MA 02115	(617) 735-9985
Fitchburg State College	Fitchburg, MA 01420-2697	(617) 345-2151
Framingham State College	Framingham, MA 01701	(508) 626-4614
MA Institute of Technology	Cambridge, MA 02139	(617) 253-4497
Massachusetts Maritime Academy	Buzzards Bay, MA 02532	(617) 759-5761
Mount Holyoke College	South Hadley, MA 01075	(413) 538-2310
Nichols College	Dudley, MA 01570	(508) 943-1560
North Adams State College	North Adams, MA 01247	(413) 664-4511
Our Lady of the Elms, College of	Chicopee, MA 01013	(413) 594-2761
Pine Manor College	Chestnut Hill, MA 02167	(617) 731-7036
Regis College	Weston, MA 02193	(617) 893-1820
Salem State College	Salem, MA 01970	(508) 741-6570
Simmons College	Boston, MA 02115	(617) 738-2240
Smith College	Northampton, MA 01063	(413) 585-2701
Southeastern Massachusetts Univ.	North Dartmouth, MA 02747-2300	(508) 999-8722
Suffolk University	Boston, MA 02114	(617) 573-8379
Tufts University	Medford, MA 02155	(617) 381-3232
University of Massachusetts	Boston, MA 02125	(617) 287-7810
Wellesley College	Wellesley, MA 02181	(617) 235-0320
Wentworth Inst. of Technology	Boston, MA 02115	(617) 442-9010
Western New England College	Springfield, MA 01119	(413) 782-3111
Westfield State College	Westfield, MA 01085	(413) 568-3311
Wheaton College	Norton, MA 02766	(508) 285-7722
Williams College	Williamstown, MA 01267	(413) 597-2366
Worcester Polytechnic Institute	Worcester, MA 01609	(508) 831-5243
Worcester State College	Worcester, MA 01602-2597	(508) 793-8034

MICHIGAN

Adrian College	Adrian, MI 49221	(517) 265-5161
Albion College	Albion, MI 49224	(517) 629-0451
Alma College	Alma, MI 48801	(517) 463-7288

Calvin College	Grand Rapids, MI 49546-4388	(616) 957-6000
Hope College	Holland, MI 49423	(616) 394-7698
Kalamazoo College	Kalamazoo, MI 49007	(616) 383-8605
Olivet College	Olivet, MI 49076	(616) 749-7671

MINNESOTA

Augsburg College	Minneapolis, MN 55454	(612) 330-1241
Bethel College	St. Paul, MN 55112	(612) 638-6396
Carleton College	Northfield, MN 55057	(507) 663-4052
Concordia College	Moorhead, MN 56562-3597	(218) 299-4435
Gustavus Adolphus College	St. Peter, MN 56082	(507) 931-7622
Hamline University	St. Paul, MN 55104	(612) 641-2326
Macalester College	St. Paul, MN 55105	(612) 696-6164
St. Benedict, College of	St. Joseph, MN 56374	(612) 363-5301
St. Catherine, College of	St. Paul, MN 55105	(612) 690-6993
St. John's University	Collegeville, MN 56321	(612) 363-3387
St. Mary's College	Winona, MN 55987	(507) 457-1578
St. Olaf College	Northfield, MN 55057	(507) 663-3253
St. Scholastica, College of	Duluth, MN 55811	(218) 723-6199
University of St. Thomas	St. Paul, MN 55105	(612) 647-5356

MISSISSIPPI

Millsaps College	Jackson, MS 39210	(601) 354-5229
Rust College	Holly Springs, MS 38635	(601) 252-4661

MISSOURI

Maryville College	St. Louis, MO 63141	(314) 576-9484
Washington University	St. Louis, MO 63130	(314) 889-5288
Webster University	Webster Groves, MO 63119	(314) 968-6984

NEBRASKA

Nebraska Wesleyan University	Lincoln, NE 68504	(402) 465-2223

NEW HAMPSHIRE

Colby-Sawyer College	New London, NH 03257	(603) 526-2010
Daniel Webster College	Nashua, NH 03063-1699	(603) 883-3556
New England College	Henniker, NH 03242-3293	(603) 428-2292
Plymouth State College	Plymouth, NH 03264	(603) 536-5000

NEW JERSEY

Drew University	Madison, NJ 07940	(201) 408-3648
Fairleigh Dickinson University	Madison, NJ 07940	(201) 593-8960
Glassboro State College	Glassboro, NJ 08028-1743	(609) 863-5365
Jersey City State College	Jersey City, NJ 07305-1597	(201) 547-3317
Kean College	Union, NJ 07083	(201) 527-2435
Montclair State College	Upper Montclair, NJ 07043	(201) 893-5234
NJ Institute of Technology	Newark, NJ 07102	(201) 596-3635
Ramapo College	Mahwah, NJ 07430	(201) 529-7675
Rutgers University	Camden, NJ 08102	(609) 757-6193
Rutgers University	Newark, NJ 07102	(201) 648-5474 Div. I in men's volleyball
St. Elizabeth, College of	Convent Station, NJ 07961	(201) 292-6367
Stevens Institute of Technology	Hoboken, NJ 07030	(201) 420-5692
Stockton State College	Pomona, NJ 08240	(609) 652-4217
Trenton State College	Trenton, NJ 08625-4700	(609) 771-2230

Upsala College	East Orange, NJ 07019-1186	(201) 266-7277	
William Paterson College	Wayne, NJ 07470	(201) 595-2356	

NEW YORK

Albany, State Univ. of New York at	Albany, NY 12222	(518) 442-3076	
Alfred University	Alfred, NY 14802	(607) 871-2193	
Bernard M. Baruch College	New York, NY 10010	(212) 387-1271	
Binghamton, State Univ. of NY at	Binghamton, NY 13902-6000	(607) 777-4255	
Brockport State University College	Brockport, NY 14420	(716) 395-2579	
Buffalo State College	Buffalo, NY 14222	(716) 878-6533	
Clarkson University	Potsdam, NY 13699	(315) 268-6616	Div. I in ice hockey
Cortland State University College	Cortland, NY 13045	(607) 753-4963	
Elmira College	Elmira, NY 14901	(607) 734-3911	
Fredonia State University College	Fredonia, NY 14063	(716) 673-3102	
Geneseo State University College	Geneseo, NY 14454	(716) 245-5345	
Hamilton College	Clinton, NY 13323	(315) 859-4115	
Hartwick College	Oneonta, NY 13820	(607) 431-4702	Div. I in men's soccer
Hobart and William Smith Colleges	Geneva, NY 14456	(315) 789-6822	
Hunter College	New York, NY 10021	(212) 772-4783	
Ithaca College	Ithaca, NY 14850	(607) 274-3209	
John Jay Coll. of Criminal Justice	Mew York, NY 10019	(212) 237-8371	
Keuka College	Keuka Park, NY 14478	(315) 536-4411	
Lehman College	Bronx, NY 10468	(212) 960-8101	
Manhattanville College	Purchase, NY 10577	(914) 694-2200	
Medgar Evers College	Brooklyn, NY 11225	(718) 270-6402	
Mount St. Mary's College	Newburgh, NY 12550	(914) 561-8000	
Mount St. Vincent, College of	Riverdale, NY 10471-1093	(212) 549-8000	
Nazareth College	Rochester, NY 14610	(716) 586-2525	
New Paltz State University College	New Paltz, NY 12561	(914) 257-3923	
New Rochelle, College of	New Rochelle, NY 10801	(914) 654-5315	
New York, City College of	New York, NY 10031	(212) 650-7550	
New York Maritime College	Bronx, NY 10465	(212) 409-7330	
New York University	New York, NY 10012-1019	(212) 998-2040	
Oneonta State University College	Oneonta, NY 13820	(607) 431-3594	Div. I in men's soccer
Oswego State University College	Oswego, NY 13126	(315) 341-2378	
Plattsburgh State Univ. College	Plattsburgh, NY 12901	(518) 564-3140	
Polytechnic University	Brooklyn, NY 11201	(718) 260-3860	
Potsdam State University College	Potsdam, NY 13676	(315) 267-2308	
Rensselaer Polytechnic Institute	Troy, NY 12181	(518) 176-6685	Div. I in ice hockey
Rochester Institute of Technology	Rochester, NY 14623	(716) 475-2615	
St. John Fisher College	Rochester, NY 14618	(716) 385-8310	
St. Lawrence University	Canton, NY 13617	(315) 379-5875	Div. I in ice hockey
Skidmore College	Saratoga Springs, NY 12866	(518) 584-5000	
Staten Island, College of	Staten Island, NY 10301	(718) 390-7607	
Stony Brook, State Univ. of NY	Stony Brook, NY 11794	(516) 632-7210	Div. I in men's lacrosse women's soccer
U.S. Merchant Marine Academy	King's Point, NY 11024-1699	(516) 773-5454	
Union College	Schenectady, NY 12308	(518) 370-6284	
University of Rochester	Rochester, NY 14627	(716) 275-4301	
Utica College	Utica, NY 13502	(315) 792-3051	
Utica/Rome, SUNY Inst. of Tech	Utica, NY 13504-3050	(315) 792-7520	
Vassar College	Poughkeepsie, NY 12601	(914) 437-7458	
Wells College	Aurora, NY 13026-0500	(315) 364-3249	
Yeshiva University	New York, NY 10033	(212) 960-5211	

NORTH CAROLINA

Greensboro College	Greensboro, NC 27401-1875	(919) 271-2235
Guilford College	Greensboro, NC 27410	(919) 292-5511
Meredith College	Raleigh, NC 27607-5298	(919) 829-8309
Methodist College	Fayetteville, NC 28311	(919) 488-7110
North Carolina Wesleyan College	Rocky Mount, NC 27804	(919) 977-7171

OHIO

Baldwin-Wallace College	Berea, OH 44017	(216) 826-2184
Bluffton College	Bluffton, OH 45817	(419) 358-8015
Capital University	Columbus, OH 43209-2394	(614) 236-6911
Case Western Reserve University	Cleveland, OH 44106	(216) 368-2866
Denison University	Granville, OH 43023	(614) 587-6581
Heidelberg College	Tiffin, OH 44883	(419) 448-2019
Hiram College	Hiram, OH 44234-0067	(216) 569-5345
John Carroll University	University Heights, OH 44118	(216) 397-4497
Kenyon College	Gambier, OH 43022	(614) 427-5811
Marietta College	Marietta, OH 45750	(614) 374-4667
Mount Union College	Alliance, OH 44601	(216) 821-5320
Muskingum College	New Concord, OH 43762	(614) 826-8320
Oberlin College	Oberlin, OH 44074	(216) 775-8502
Ohio Northern University	Ada, OH 45810	(419) 772-2443
Ohio Wesleyan University	Delaware, OH 43015	(614) 368-3727
Otterbein College	Westerville, OH 43081	(614) 898-1653
Wilmington College	Wilmington, OH 45177	(513) 382-6661
Wittenberg University	Springfield, OH 45501-0720	(513) 327-6450
Wooster, College of	Wooster, OH 44691	(216) 263-2189

PENNSYLVANIA

Albright College	Reading, PA 19603	(215) 921-2381	
Allegheny College	Meadville, PA 16335	(814) 332-5372	
Allentown Col\St. Francis de Sales	Center Valley, PA 18034	(215) 282-1100	
Bryn Mawr College	Bryn Mawr, PA 19010-2899	(215) 526-5364	
Cabrini College	Radnor, PA 19087	(215) 971-8386	
Carnegie Mellon University	Pittsburgh, PA 15213	(412) 268-2211	
Delaware Valley College	Doylestown, PA 18901-2699	(215) 345-1500	
Dickinson College	Carlisle, PA 17013	(717) 245-1320	
Elizabethtown College	Elizabethtown, PA 17022-2298	(717) 367-1151	
Franklin and Marshall College	Lancaster, PA 17604-3003	(717) 291-4104	Div. I in wrestling
Gettysburg College	Gettysburg, PA 17325	(717) 337-6400	
Grove City College	Grove City, PA 16127	(415) 458-2120	
Haverford College	Haverford, PA 19041	(215) 896-1117	
Immaculata College	Immaculata, PA 19345	(215) 647-4400	
Juniata College	Huntingdon, PA 16652	(814) 643-4310	
King's College	Wilkes-Barre, PA 18711	(717) 826-5855	
Lebanon Valley College	Annville, PA 17003	(717) 867-6261	
Lincoln University	Lincoln University, PA 19352	(215) 932-8300	
Lycoming College	Williamsport, PA 17701	(717) 321-4260	
Marywood College	Scranton, PA 18509	(717) 348-6259	
Messiah College	Grantham, PA 17027	(717) 691-6018	
Moravian College	Bethlehem, PA 18018	(215) 861-1534	
Muhlenberg College	Allentown, PA 18104	(215) 821-3380	
Penn State-Behrend College	Erie, PA 16563-0101	(814) 898-6322	
Susquehanna University	Selinsgrove, PA 17870	(717) 372-4272	
Swarthmore College	Swarthmore, PA 19081	(215) 328-8222	
Thiel College	Greenville, PA 16125	(412) 589-2142	

University of Scranton	Scranton, PA 18510	(717) 941-7440	
Ursinus College	Collegeville, PA 19426	(215) 489-4111	Div. I in field hockey
Washington and Jefferson University	Washington, PA 15301	(412) 222-4400	
Waynesburg College	Waynesburg, PA 15370	(412) 627-8191	
Widener University	Chester, PA 19013	(215) 499-4443	
Wilkes University	Wilkes-Barre, PA 18766	(717) 824-4651	Div. I in wrestling
York College	York, PA 17403	(717) 846-7788	

PUERTO RICO

American University of Puerto Rico	Bayamon, PR 00621	(809) 798-2040

RHODE ISLAND

Rhode Island College	Providence, RI 02908	(401) 456-8007
Roger Williams College	Bristol, RI 02809	(401) 253-1040
Salve Regina College	Newport, RI 02840	(401) 847-6650

TENNESSEE

Fisk University	Nashville, TN 37208-3051	(615) 329-8782
Maryville College	Maryville, TN 37801	(615) 981-8287
Rhodes College	Memphis, TN 38112	(901) 726-3940
University of the South	Sewanee, TN 37375	(615) 598-1388

TEXAS

Trinity College	San Antonio, TX 78212	(512) 736-8272	Div. I in men's and women's tennis

VERMONT

Castleton State College	Castleton, VT 05735	(802) 468-5611
Johnson State College	Johnson, VT 05656	(802) 635-2356
Middlebury College	Middlebury, VT 05753	(802) 388-3711
Norwich University	Northfield, VT 05663	(802) 485-2000

VIRGINIA

Averitt College	Danville, VA 24541	(804) 791-5701
Bridgewater College	Bridgewater, VA 22812	(703) 828-2501
Christopher Newport College	Newport News, VA 23606	(804) 594-7217
Eastern Mennonite College	Harrisonburg, VA 22801	(703) 433-2771
Emory and Henry College	Emory, VA 24327	(703) 944-3121
Ferrum College	Ferrum, VA 24088	(703) 365-4496
Hampden-Sydney College	Hampden-Sydney, VA 23943	(804) 223-4381
Hollins College	Hollins College, VA 24020	(703) 362-6435
Lynchburg College	Lynchburg, VA 24501-3199	(804) 522-8498
Mary Baldwin College	Staunton, VA 24401	(703) 887-7161
Mary Washington College	Fredericksburg, VA 22401-5358	(703) 899-4044
Marymount College	Arlington, VA 22207-4229	(703) 284-1633
Randolph-Macon College	Ashland, VA 23005	(804) 752-7299
Randolph-Macon Woman's College	Lynchburg, VA 24503-1526	(804) 846-7392
Roanoke College	Salem, VA 24153	(703) 375-2337
Shenandoah College	Winchester, VA 22601	(703) 665-4566
Sweet Briar College	Sweet Briar, VA 24595	(804) 381-6149
Virginia Wesleyan College	Norfolk, VA 23502-5599	(804) 455-3302
Washington and Lee University	Lexington, VA 24450	(703) 463-8671

WEST VIRGINIA

Bethany College	Bethany, WV 26032	(304) 829-7251

WISCONSIN

Beloit College	Beloit, WI 53511	(608) 363-2234
Carroll College	Waukesha, WI 53186-5593	(414) 547-1211
Carthage College	Kenosha, WI 53140	(414) 551-8500
Lawrence University	Appleton, WI 54912	(414) 735-6763
Northwestern College	Watertown, WI 53094	(414) 261-0806
Ripon College	Ripon, WI 54971	(414) 748-8331
St. Norbert College	De Pere, WI 54115	(414) 337-3030
University of Wisconsin	Eau Claire, WI 54702-4004	(715) 836-4183
University of Wisconsin	La Crosse, WI 54601	(608) 785-8617
University of Wisconsin	Oshkosh, WI 54901-8617	(414) 424-1034
University of Wisconsin	Platteville, WI 53818-3099	(608) 341-1567
University of Wisconsin	River Falls, WI 54022	(715) 425-3900
University of Wisconsin	Stevens Point, WI 54481	(715) 346-3888
University of Wisconsin, Stout	Menomonie, WI 54751	(715) 232-2116
University of Wisconsin	Superior, WI 54880	(715) 394-8371
University of Wisconsin	Whitewater, WI 53190	(414) 472-4661

NAIA

The National Association of Intercollegiate Athletics includes more than 480 four-year colleges and universities. There is no limit on the number of athletic scholarships, but many are small schools with budget limitations. The country is divided into districts, with play-offs leading to national championships in 11 men's sports and nine women's sports. Conferences can choose to compete in football at either the Division I or Division II level, and a similar two-division breakdown for basketball begins in the 1991-92 school year.

CANADA
Simon Fraser University	Burnaby, BC, Can V5A 1S6	(604) 291-3313

ALABAMA
Athens State College	Athens, AL 35611	(205) 233-8279
Auburn U. at Montgomery	Montgomery, AL 36117-3596	(205) 244-3541
Birmingham-Southern College	Birmingham, AL 35254	(205) 226-4640
Faulkner University	Montgomery, AL 36193	(205) 272-5820
Huntingdon College	Montgomery, AL 36194-6201	(205) 265-0511
Mobile College	Mobile, AL 36613	(205) 675-5990
Selma University	Selma, AL 36701	(205) 872-2533
Spring Hill College	Mobile, AL 36608	(205) 460-2346
Talladega College	Talladega, AL 35160	(205) 362-0206
University of Montevallo	Montevallo, Ala 35115-6591	(205) 665-6591

ALASKA
Sheldon Jackson College	Sitka, AK 99835	(907) 747-5271

ARIZONA
Embry-Riddle Aeronautical Univ.	Prescott, AZ 86301	(602) 776-3728
Grand Canyon University	Phoenix, AZ 85017-1097	(602) 249-3300

ARKANSAS
Arkansas Baptist College	Little Rock, AR 72202	(501) 374-7856
Arkansas College	Batesville, AR 72501	(501) 698-4221
Arkansas Tech University	Russellville, AR 72801-2222	(501) 968-0345
Harding University	Searcy, AR 72143-5590	(501) 279-4249
Henderson State University	Arkadelphia, AR 71923	(501) 246-5511
Hendrix College	Conway, AR 72032-3002	(501) 450-1313
John Brown University	Siloam Springs, AR 72761	(501) 524-3131
Ouchatia Baptist University	Arkadelphia, AR 71923	(501) 246-4531
Philander Smith College	Little Rock, AR 72202	(501) 375-9845
Southern Arkansas University	Magnolia, AR 71753	(501) 235-4102
Univ. of Arkansas at Little Rock	Little Rock, AR 72204	(501) 569-3167
Univ. of Arkansas at Monticello	Monticello, AR 71655	(501) 460-1058
Univ. of Arkansas at Pine Bluff	Pine Bluff, AR 71601	(501) 541-6585
University of Central Arkansas	Conway, AR 72032	(501) 450-3150
University of the Ozarks	Clarksville, AR 72830	(501) 754-3839
Williams Baptist College	College City, AR 72476	(501) 886-6741

CALIFORNIA

Azusa Pacific University	Azusa, CA 91702-7000	(818) 969-3434
Bethany Coll/the Assemblies of God	Scotts Valley, CA 95060	(408) 438-3800
Biola University	La Mirada, CA 90639	(213) 903-4886
California Baptist College	Riverside, CA 92504	(714) 689-5771
California Lutheran University	Thousand Oaks, CA 91360	(805) 493-3402
Christ College Irvine	Irvine, CA 92715	(714) 854-8002
Christian Heritage College	El Cajon, CA 92019	(619) 440-3043
Dominican College	San Raphael, CA 94901-8008	(415) 485-3230
Fresno Pacific College	Fresno, CA 93702	(209) 453-2086
The Master's College	Newhall, CA 91321	(805) 259-3540
Mount Saint Mary's College	Los Angeles, CA 90049-1597	(213) 476-2237
Point Loma Nazarene College	San Diego, CA 92106-2899	(619) 221-2266
Southern California College	Costa Mesa, CA 92626	(714) 556-3610
Westmont College	Santa Barbara, CA 93108-1099	(805) 565-6010

COLORADO

Adams State College	Alamosa, CO 81102	(719) 589-7401
Colorado School of Mines	Golden, CO 80401	(303) 273-3368
Fort Lewis College	Durango, CO 81301	(303) 247-7371
Mesa State College	Grand Junction, CO 81501	(303) 248-1503
U of Colorado at Colorado Springs	Colorado Springs, CO 80933-7150	(719) 593-3575
University of Southern Colorado	Pueblo, CO 81001-4901	(719) 549-2711
Western State College of CO	Gunnison, CO 81231	(303) 943-2079

CONNECTICUT

Teikyo Post University	Waterbury, CT 06723-2540	(203) 755-0121

DELAWARE

Goldey-Beacom College	Wilmington, DE 19808	(302) 998-8814
Wilmington College	New Castle, DE 19720	(302) 328-9401

FLORIDA

College of Boca Raton	Boca Raton, FL 33431-5598	(407) 994-0770
Edward Waters College	Jacksonville, FL 32209	(904) 366-2798
Embry-Riddle Aeronautical Univ.	Daytona Beach, FL 32114	(904) 239-6553
Flagler College	St. Augustine, FL 32085	(904) 829-6481
Florida Memorial College	Miami, FL 33054	(305) 625-4141
Northwood Institute	West Palm Beach, FL 33409	(407) 478-5515
Nova University	Fort Lauderdale, FL 33314	(305) 475-7345
Palm Beach Atlantic College	West Palm Beach, FL 33402	(407) 650-7727
Saint Thomas University	Miami, FL 33054	(305) 628-6677
University of North Florida	Jacksonville, FL 32216	(904) 646-2833
University of West Florida	Pensacola, FL 32514	(904) 474-3004
Warner Southern College	Lake Wales, FL 33853	(813) 638-1464
Webber College	Babson Park, FL 33827	(813) 638-1431

GEORGIA

Agnes Scott College	Decatur, GA 30030-9989	(404) 371-6358
Berry College	Rome, GA 30149	(404) 232-5374
Brenau College	Gainesville, GA 30501	(404) 534-6230
Brewton Parker College	Mount Vernon, GA 30445-0197	(912) 583-2241
Clayton State College	Morrow, GA 30260	(404) 961-3450
Covenant College	Lookout Mountain, GA 30750-9601	(404) 820-1560
DeVry Institute of Technology	Decatur, GA 30030	(404) 292-7900

Georgia College	Milledgeville, GA 31061	(912) 453-4072
Georgia Southwestern College	Americus, GA 31709	(912) 928-1262
Kennesaw State College	Marietta, GA 30061-0444	(404) 423-6284
LaGrange College	LaGrange, GA 30240	(404) 882-2911
Life College	Marietta, GA 30060	(404) 424-0554
North Georgia College	Dahlonega, GA 30597	(404) 864-1630
Piedmont College	Demorest, GA 30535	(404) 778-8346
Savannah Col. of Art and Design	Savannah, GA 31402-3146	(912) 238-2470
Shorter College	Rome, GA 30161-4298	(404) 291-2121
Southern Col. of Technology	Marietta, GA 30060-2896	(404) 528-7350

HAWAII

Brigham Young University/Hawaii	Laie, HI 96762	(808) 293-3751
Hawaii Loa College	Kaneohe, HI 96744-5297	(808) 235-3641
Hawaii Pacific University	Honolulu, HI 96813	(808) 544-0220
University of Hawaii at Hilo	Hilo, HI 96720-4091	(808) 933-3520

IDAHO

College of Idaho	Caldwell, ID 83605	(208) 459-5512
Lewis Clark State College	Lewiston, ID 83501	(208) 799-2275
Northwest Nazarene College	Nampa, ID 83686-5897	(208) 467-8348

ILLINOIS

Barat College	Lake Forest, IL 60045	(312) 234-3000
Eureka College	Eureka, IL 61530-0280	(309) 467-6373
Greenville College	Greenville, IL 62246	(618) 664-1840
Illinois Institute of Technology	Chicago, IL 60616	(312) 567-3298
Judson College	Elgin, IL 60123	(312) 695-2500
McKendree College	Lebanon, IL 62254	(618) 537-4481
Mundelein College	Chicago, IL 60660	(312) 262-7125
National-Louis University	Evanston, IL 60201	(708) 256-5150
Olivet Nazarene University	Kankakee, IL 60901	(815) 939-5123
Roosevelt University	Chicago, IL 60605	(312) 341-3597
Rosary College	River Forest, IL 60305	(312) 366-2490
College of Saint Francis	Joliet, IL 60435-6144	(815) 740-3464
Saint Xavier College	Chicago, IL 60655	(312) 779-3300
Sangamon State University	Springfield, IL 62794-9243	(217) 786-6674
Trinity Christian College	Palos Heights, IL 60463	(312) 597-3000
Trinity College	Deerfield, IL 60015	(708) 317-7091

INDIANA

Anderson University	Anderson, IN 46012-3462	(317) 641-4483
Bethel College	Mishawaka, IN 46545	(219) 259-8511
DePauw University	Greencastle, IN 46135	(317) 658-4935
Franklin College	Franklin, IN 46131-2598	(317) 736-8441
Goshen College	Goshen, IN 46526	(219) 535-7492
Grace College	Winona Lake, IN 46590	(219) 372-5219
Hanover College	Hanover, IN 47243	(812) 866-7373
Huntingdon College	Huntingdon, IN 46750	(219) 356-6000
Indiana Institute of Technology	Fort Wayne, IN 46803	(219) 422-5561
Indiana University Southeast	New Albany, IN 47150	(812) 941-2432
Indiana University at South Bend	South Bend, IN 46634	(219) 237-4372
Indiana U-Purdue U at Indianapolis	Indianapolis, IN 46202-5193	(317) 274-2725
Indiana Wesleyan University	Marion, IN 46953-9980	(317) 677-2317
Manchester College	North Manchester, IN 46962-1299	(219) 982-5390
Marian College	Indianapolis, IN 46222	(317) 929-0370

Oakland City College	Oakland City, IN 47660	(812) 749-1290
Purdue University Calumet	Hammond, IN 46323-2094	(219) 989-2540
Saint Francis College	Fort Wayne, IN 46808	(219) 432-3551
Taylor University	Upland, IN 46989	(317) 998-5311
Tri-State University	Angola, IN 46703	(219) 665-4140

IOWA

Briar Cliff College	Sioux City, IA 51104-2100	(712) 279-1656
Clarke College	Dubuque, IA 52001	(319) 588-6570
Dordt College	Sioux Center, IA 51250	(712) 722-3771
Graceland College	Lamoni, IA 50140	(515) 784-5311
Grand View College	Des Moines, IA 50316	(515) 263-2897
Iowa Wesleyan College	Mount Pleasant, IA 52641	(319) 385-6303
Marycrest College	Davenport, IA 52804	(319) 326-9584
Mount Mercy College	Cedar Rapids, IA 52402	(319) 363-8213
Mount Saint Clare College	Clinton, IA 52732	(319) 242-4023
Northwestern College	Orange City, IA 51041-9981	(712) 737-4821
Saint Ambrose University	Davenport, IA 52803-2898	(319) 383-8727
Teikyo Westmar University	Le Mars, IA 51031	(712) 546-7081

KANSAS

Baker University	Baldwin City, KS 66006	(913) 594-6451
Benedictine College	Atchison, KS 66002-1499	(913) 367-5340
Bethany College	Lindsborg, KS 67456-1897	(913) 227-3311
Bethel College	North Newton, KS 67117-9989	(316) 283-2500
Emporia State University	Emporia, KS 66801	(316) 343-5354
Fort Hays State University	Hays, KS 67601-4099	(913) 628-4050
Friends University	Wichita, KS 67213-3397	(316) 264-9627
Kansas Newman College	Wichita, KS 67213	(316) 942-4291
Kansas Wesleyan University	Salina, KS 67401	(913) 827-5541
McPherson College	McPherson, KS 67460-1402	(316) 241-0731
MidAmerica Nazarene College	Olathe, KS 66061-1776	(913) 782-3750
Ottawa University	Ottawa, KS 66067	(913) 242-5200
Saint Mary College	Leavenworth, KS 66048	(913) 682-5151
Saint Mary of the Plains	Dodge City, KS 67801	(316) 225-4171
Southwestern College	Winfield, KS 67156-2558	(316) 221-4150
Sterling College	Sterling, KS 67579	(316) 278-2173
Tabor College	Hillsboro, KS 67063	(316) 947-3121

KENTUCKY

Alice Lloyd College	Pippa Passes, KY 41844	(606) 368-2101
Asbury College	Wilmore, KY 40390-1198	(606) 858-3511
Berea College	Berea, KY 40404	(606) 986-9341
Brescia College	Owensboro, KY 42301	(502) 686-4330
Campbellsville College	Campbellsville, KY 42718	(502) 465-8158
Cumberland College	Williamsburg, KY 40769	(606) 549-2200
Georgetown College	Georgetown, KY 40324-1696	(502) 863-8115
Lindsey Wilson College	Columbia, KY 42728	(502) 384-2126
Midway College	Midway, KY 40347-1120	(606) 846-5387
Pikeville College	Pikeville, KY 41501-1194	(606) 432-9235
Transylvania University	Lexington, KY 40502	(606) 233-8270
Union College	Barbourville, KY 40906	(606) 546-4151

LOUISIANA

Centenary College	Shreveport, LA 71134-1188	(318) 869-5087
Dillard University	New Orleans, LA 70122-3097	(504) 286-4644

103

Louisiana College	Pineville, LA 71359	(318) 487-7322
Loyola University	New Orleans, LA 70118	(504) 865-3137
Southern Univ. at New Orleans	New Orleans, LA 70126	(504) 286-5195
Xavier University of Louisiana	New Orleans, LA 70125	(504) 483-7329

MAINE

Husson College	Bangor, ME 04401	(207) 947-1121
Saint Joseph's College	Windham, ME 04062	(207) 892-6766
Thomas College	Waterville, ME 04901	(207) 873-0771
Unity College	Unity, ME 04988	(207) 948-3131
University of Maine at Augusta	Augusta, ME 04330-9410	(207) 622-7131
University of Maine at Farmington	Farmington, ME 04938	(207) 778-3501
University of Maine at Fort Kent	Fort Kent, ME 04743	(207) 834-3162
University of Maine at Machias	Machias, ME 04654	(207) 255-3313
University of Maine at Presque Isle	Presque Isle, ME 04769	(207) 764-0311
University of New England	Biddeford, ME 04005	(207) 283-0171

MARYLAND

Capitol College	Lauren, MD 20708	(301) 953-0060
Columbia Union College	Takoma Park, MD 20912	(301) 891-4024

MASSACHUSETTS

Atlantic Union College	South Lancaster, MA 01561	(508) 368-2141
Eastern Nazarene College	Wollaston, MA 02170	(617) 773-6350

MICHIGAN

Aquinas College	Grand Rapids, MI 49506-1799	(616) 459-8281
Concordia College	Ann Arbor, MI 48105	(313) 995-7300
Detroit College of Business	Detroit, MI 48126-3799	(313) 581-4400
Grand Rapids Baptist College	Grand Rapids, MI 49505	(616) 949-5300
Hillsdale College	Hillsdale, MI 49242-1361	(517) 437-7364
Madonna College	Livonia, MI 48150-1173	(313) 591-5138
Northwood Institute	Midland, MI 48640-2398	(517) 832-4381
Saint Mary's College	Orchard Lake, MI 48033	(313) 683-0329
Siena Heights College	Adrian, MI 49221	(517) 263-0731
Spring Arbor College	Spring Arbor, MI 49283	(517) 750-1200
University of Michigan-Dearborn	Dearborn, MI 48128	(313) 593-5540

MINNESOTA

Bemidji State University	Bemidji, MN 56601-2699	(218) 755-3185
Concordia College-St. Paul	St. Paul, MN 55104-5494	(612) 641-8485
Moorhead State University	Moorhead, MN 56560	(218) 236-2325
College of Saint Scholastica	Duluth, MN 55811	(218) 723-6199
Southwest State University	Marshall, MN 56258	(507) 537-7255
University of Minnesota-Duluth	Duluth, MN 55812-2496	(218) 726-8168
University of Minnesota-Morris	Morris, MN 56267	(612) 589-2211
Winona State University	Winona, MN 55987	(507) 457-5212

MISSISSIPPI

Belhaven College	Jackson, MS 39202	(601) 968-5982
Blue Mountain College	Blue Mountain, MS 38610	(601) 685-4771
Tougaloo College	Tougaloo, MS 39174	(601) 977-7809
William Carey College	Hattiesburg, MS 39401	(601) 582-6111

MISSOURI

Avila College	Kansas City, MO 64145	(816) 942-8400
Central Methodist College	Fayette, MO 65248-1198	(816) 248-3391
College of the Ozarks	Point Lookout, MO 65726	(417) 334-6411
Columbia College	Columbia, MO 65216	(314) 875-7410
Culver-Stockton College	Canton, MO 63435	(314) 288-5221
Drury College	Springfield, MO 65802	(417) 865-8731
Evangel College	Springfield, MO 65802	(417) 865-2811
Fontbonne College	St. Louis, MO 63105-3098	(314) 889-1444
Hannibal-LaGrange College	Hannibal, MO 63401	(314) 221-3675
Harris Stowe State College	St. Louis, MO 63103	(314) 533-3366
Lindenwood College	St. Charles, MO 63301	(314) 949-2000
Missouri Baptist College	St. Louis, MO 63141	(314) 434-1115
Missouri Valley College	Marshall, MO 65340-3012	(816) 886-6924
Park College	Parkville, MO 64152-3795	(816) 741-2000
Rockhurst College	Kansas City, MO 64110-2508	(816) 926-4141
Westminster College	Fulton, MO 65251	(314) 642-3361
William Jewell College	Liberty, MO 64068	(816) 781-7700
William Woods College	Fulton, MO 65251-1098	(314) 642-2251

MONTANA

Carroll College	Helena, MT 59625	(406) 442-3450
MT C. of Mineral Science & Tech	Butte, MT 59701	(406) 496-4292
Northern Montana College	Havre, MT 59501	(406) 265-3761
Rocky Mountain College	Billings, MT 59102	(406) 657-1124
Western Montana College	Dillon, MT 59725	(406) 683-7509

NEBRASKA

Bellevue College	Bellevue, NE 68005	(402) 293-3784
Chadron State College	Chadron, NE 69337-2690	(308) 432-6345
Concordia College	Seward, NE 68434	(402) 643-7334
Dana College	Blair, NE 68008	(402) 426-7293
Doane College	Crete, NE 68333	(402) 826-8281
Hastings College	Hastings, NE 68901	(402) 463-2402
Midland Lutheran College	Fremont, NE 68025-9915	(402) 721-5480
Nebraska Wesleyan University	Lincoln, NE 68504	(402) 465-2360
Peru State College	Peru, NE 68421	(402) 872-3815
College of Saint Mary	Omaha, NE 68124	(402) 399-2451
Wayne State College	Wayne, NE 68787	(402) 375-7520

NEW JERSEY

Bloomfield College	Bloomfield, NJ 07003	(201) 748-9000
Caldwell College	Caldwell, NJ 07006-6195	(201) 228-4424
Georgian Court College	Lakewood, NJ 08701	(201) 363-2374

NEW MEXICO

College of the Southwest	Hobbs, NM 88240	(505) 392-6561
New Mexico Highlands University	Las Vegas, NM 87701	(505) 454-3351
Western New Mexico University	Silver City, NM 88061	(505) 538-6218

NEW YORK

Bard College	Annandale-on-Hudson, NY 12504	(914) 758-7528
Daemen College	Amherst, NY 14226-3592	(716) 839-3600
Dominican College	Orangeburg, NY 10962	(914) 359-6827

Houghton College	Houghton, NY 14744-0128	(716) 567-9364
The King's College	Briarcliff Manor, NY 10510-9985	(914) 944-5554
Nyack College	Nyack, NY 10960	(914) 358-1710
Saint Joseph's College-New York	Patchogue, NY 11772	(516) 654-3200
The College of Saint Rose	Albany, NY 12203	(518) 454-5282
Saint Thomas Aquinas College	Sparkill, NY 10976	(914) 359-9500

NORTH CAROLINA

Atlantic Christian College	Wilson, NC 27893-3117	(919) 237-3161
Barber-Scotia College	Concord, NC 28025	(704) 786-5171
Barton College	Wilson, NC 27893	(919) 399-6300
Belmont Abbey College	Belmont, NC 28012	(704) 825-6800
Catawba College	Salisbury, NC 28144-2488	(704) 637-4474
Elon College	Elon College, NC 27244	(919) 584-2420
Gardner-Webb College	Boiling Springs, NC 28017	(704) 434-2361
Guilford College	Greensboro, NC 27410	(919) 292-5511
High Point College	High Point, NC 27261	(919) 841-9275
Lenoir-Rhyne College	Hickory, NC 28603	(704) 328-7114
Mars Hill College	Mars Hill, NC 28754	(704) 689-1368
Mount Olive College	Mount Olive, NC 28365	(919) 658-5056
Pembroke State University	Pembroke, NC 28372-1510	(919) 521-9481
Pfeiffer College	Misenheimer, NC 28109	(704) 463-1360
Saint Andrew's Presbyterian College	Laurinberg, NC 28352	(919) 276-3652
Warren Wilson College	Swannanoa, NC 28778	(704) 298-3325
Wingate College	Wingate, NC 28174-0157	(704) 233-8193

NORTH DAKOTA

Dickinson State University	Dickinson, ND 58601-4896	(701) 227-2159
Jamestown College	Jamestown, ND 58401	(701) 252-3467
Mayville State University	Mayville, ND 58257-1299	(701) 786-4835
Minot State University	Minot, ND 58702-5002	(701) 857-3042
University of Mary	Bismarck, ND 58504	(701) 255-7500
Valley City State University	Valley City, ND 58072	(701) 845-7161

OHIO

Bluffton College	Bluffton, OH 45817	(419) 358-8015
Cedarville College	Cedarville, OH 45314-0601	(513) 766-2211
Central State University	Wilberforce, OH 45384	(513) 376-6319
Defiance College	Defiance, OH 43512	(419) 784-4010
Dyke College	Cleveland, OH 44115	(216) 696-9000
Lake Erie College	Painesville, OH 44007	(216) 352-3361
Malone College	Canton, OH 44709-3897	(216) 489-7376
College of Mount Saint Joseph	Mount Saint Joseph, OH 45051	(513) 244-4311
Mount Vernon Nazarene College	Mount Vernon, OH 43050	(614) 397-1244
Notre Dame College of Ohio	Cleveland, OH 44121	(216) 381-1680
Ohio Dominican College	Columbus, OH 43219	(614) 251-4535
Shawnee State University	Portsmouth, OH 45662	(614) 355-2219
Tiffin University	Tiffin, OH 44883	(419) 447-6444
University of Findlay	Findlay, OH 45840	(419) 424-4663
University of Rio Grande	Rio Grande, OH 45674	(614) 245-5353
Urbana University	Urbana, OH 43078	(513) 652-1301
Walsh College	Canton, OH 44720	(216) 499-7090
Wilberforce University	Wilberforce, OH 45384	(513) 376-2911
Wilmington College	Wilmington, OH 45177	(513) 382-6661

OKLAHOMA

Bartlesville Wesleyan College	Bartlesville, OK 74006	(918) 333-6151
East Central University	Ada, OK 74820-6899	(405) 332-8000
Langston University	Langston, OK 73050	(405) 466-2231
Northeastern Oklahoma State U.	Tahlequah, OK 74464	(918) 456-5511
Northwestern Oklahoma State U.	Alva, OK 73717	(405) 327-1700
Oklahoma Baptist University	Shawnee, OK 74801	(405) 878-2132
Oklahoma Christian University	Oklahoma City, OK 73136-1100	(405) 425-5352
Oklahoma City University	Oklahoma City, OK 73106-1498	(405) 521-5302
Oral Roberts University	Tulsa, OK 74171	(918) 495-7177
Panhandle State University	Goodwell, OK 73939	(405) 349-2611
Phillips University	Enid, OK 73702	(405) 237-4433
Southeastern Oklahoma State U.	Durant, OK 74701	(405) 924-0121
Southern Nazarene University	Bethany, OK 73008	(405) 789-6339
Southwestern Oklahoma State U.	Weatherford, OK 73096	(405) 774-3182
U. of Science & Arts of Oklahoma	Chickasha, OK 73018	(405) 224-3140

OREGON

Columbia Christian College	Portland, OR 97216	(503) 257-1259
Concordia College	Portland, OR 97211	(503) 280-8516
Eastern Oregon State College	LaGrande, OR 97850	(503) 962-3363
George Fox College	Newberg, OR 97132	(503) 538-8383
Lewis and Clark College	Portland, OR 97219	(503) 293-2707
Linfield College	McMinnville, OR 97128-6894	(503) 472-4121
Oregon Institute of Technology	Klamath Falls, OR 97601-8801	(503) 882-6366
Pacific University	Forest Grove, OR 97116	(503) 357-6151
Southern Oregon State College	Ashland, OR 97520	(503) 482-6236
Warner Pacific College	Portland, OR 97215	(503) 775-4366
Western Baptist College	Salem, OR 97301	(503) 581-8600
Western Oregon State College	Monmouth, OR 97361	(503) 838-8252
Willamette University	Salem, OR 97301	(503) 370-6217

PENNSYLVANIA

Alvernia College	Reading, PA 19607	(215) 777-5411
Beaver College	Glenside, PA 19038	(215) 572-2996
Carlow College	Pittsburgh, PA 15213	(412) 578-6000
Cedar Crest College	Allentown, PA 18104-6196	(215) 437-4471
College Misercordia	Dallas, PA 18612	(717) 674-6294
Eastern College	St. Davids, PA 19087	(215) 341-1738
Geneva College	Beaver Falls, PA 15010	(412) 847-6655
Gwynedd Mercy College	Gwynedd Valley, PA 19437	(215) 641-5575
Holy Family College	Philadelphia, PA 19114	(215) 632-8284
La Roche College	Pittsburgh, PA 15237	(412) 367-9275
Neumann College	Aston, PA 19014-1297	(215) 558-5627
Penn State U. at Harrisburg	Middletown, PA 17057	(717) 948-6266
Phil. C. of Pharmacy & Science	Philadelphia, PA 19104-4495	(215) 596-8916
Point Park College	Pittsburgh, PA 15222	(412) 392-3844
Saint Vincent College	Latrobe, PA 15650-2690	(412) 537-4564
Seton Hill College	Greensburg, PA 15601	(412) 834-2200
U. of Pittsburgh at Bradford	Bradford, PA 16701-2898	(814) 362-7520
Westminster College	New Wilmington, PA 16172	(412) 946-7308
Wilson College	Chambersburg, PA 17201	(717) 264-4141

SOUTH CAROLINA

Benedict College	Columbia, SC 29204	(803) 733-8334
Central Wesleyan College	Central, SC 29630	(803) 639-2453

Claflin College	Orangeburg, SC 29115	(803) 534-2710
Coker College	Hartsville, SC 29550-3797	(803) 383-8074
Columbia College	Columbia, SC 29203	(803) 786-3723
Converse College	Spartanburg, SC 29302-0006	(803) 596-9149
Erskine College	Due West, SC 29639	(803) 379-8701
Francis Marion College	Florence, SC 29501	(803) 661-1240
Lander College	Greenwood, SC 29649	(803) 229-8314
Limestone College	Gaffney, SC 29702	(803) 489-7151
Morris College	Sumter, SC 29150	(803) 775-9371
Newberry College	Newberry, SC 29108	(803) 276-5010
Presbyterian College	Clinton, SC 29325	(803) 833-8242
University of South Carolina/Aiken	Aiken, SC 29801	(803) 648-6851
Voorhees College	Denmark, SC 29042-0678	(803) 793-3351

SOUTH DAKOTA

Black Hills State College	Spearfish, SD 57799-9504	(605) 642-6882
Dakota State University	Madison, SD 57042-1799	(605) 256-5233
Dakota Wesleyan University	Mitchell, SD 57301-4398	(605) 995-2875
Huron College	Huron, SD 57350	(605) 352-8721
Mount Marty College	Yankton, SD 57078	(605) 668-1541
National College	Rapid City, SD 57701	(605) 394-4979
Northern State College	Aberdeen, SD 57401	(605) 622-2488
Sioux Falls College	Sioux Falls, SD 57105-1699	(605) 331-6655
South Dakota Tech	Rapid City, SD 55701-3995	(605) 394-2352

TENNESSEE

Belmont College	Nashville, TN 37212-3757	(615) 385-6420
Bethel College	McKenzie, TN 38201	(901) 352-5462
Bryan College	Dayton, TN 37321	(615) 775-2041
Carson-Newman College	Jefferson City, TN 37760	(615) 475-9061
Christian Brothers College	Memphis, TN 38104	(901) 722-0374
Cumberland University	Lebanon, TN 37087	(615) 444-2562
David Lipscomb University	Nashville, TN 37204-3951	(615) 269-1000
Freed-Hardeman College	Henderson, TN 38340	(901) 989-6046
King College	Bristol, TN 37620	(615) 968-1187
Knoxville College	Knoxville, TN 37921	(615) 524-6519
Lambuth College	Jackson, TN 38301	(901) 425-3231
Lee College	Cleveland, TN 37311	(615) 478-7363
Lincoln Memorial University	Harrogate, TN 37752-0901	(615) 869-6238
Milligan College	Milligan College, TN 37682	(615) 929-0116
Tennessee Wesleyan College	Athens, TN 37303	(615) 745-7504
Trevecca Nazarene College	Nashville, TN 37210-2877	(615) 248-1271
Tusculum College	Greeneville, TN 37743-9997	(615) 636-7300
Union University	Jackson, TN 38305	(901) 668-1818

TEXAS

Austin College	Sherman, TX 75091-1177	(214) 813-2272
Concordia Lutheran College	Austin, TX 78705	(512) 452-7661
Dallas Baptist University	Dallas, TX 75211-9800	(214) 333-5326
East Texas Baptist University	Marshall, TX 75670	(214) 935-7963
Hardin-Simmons University	Abilene, TX 79698	(915) 670-1435
Houston Baptist University	Houston, TX 77074-3298	(713) 995-3314
Howard Payne University	Brownwood, TX 76801	(915) 646-2502
Huston-Tillotson College	Austin, TX 78702	(512) 476-7421
Incarnate Word College	San Antonio, TX 78209	(512) 828-1261
Jarvis Christian College	Hawkins, TX 75765	(214) 769-2174

LeTourneau University	Longview, TX 75602	(214) 753-0231
Lubbock Christian University	Lubbock, TX 79407-2099	(806) 796-8800
McMurry College	Abilene, TX 79697	(915) 691-6274
Midwestern State University	Wichita Falls, TX 76308-2099	(817) 692-6611
Northwood Institute	Cedar Hill, TX 75104	(214) 291-1541
Prairie View A&M University	Prairie View, TX 77446-0097	(409) 857-4319
Saint Edward's University	Austin, TX 78704	(512) 448-8450
Saint Mary's University	San Antonio, TX 78284-0400	(512) 436-3528
Schreiner College	Kerrville, TX 78028	(512) 896-5411
Southwestern University	Georgetown, TX 78627-9986	(512) 863-1381
Sul Ross State University	Alpine, TX 79832	(915) 837-8226
Tarleton State University	Stephenville, TX 76402	(817) 968-9177
Texas College	Tyler, TX 75702	(214) 593-8311
Texas Lutheran College	Seguin, TX 78155-5999	(512) 372-8120
Texas Wesleyan University	Fort Worth, TX 76105-1536	(817) 531-4879
University of Dallas	Irving, TX 75062-4799	(214) 721-5207
University of Mary Hardin-Baylor	Belton, TX 76513	(817) 939-4617
Univ. of Texas at Tyler	Tyler, TX 75701-6699	(214) 566-7105
Wayland Baptist University	Plainview, TX 79072	(806) 296-5521
Wiley College	Marshall, TX 75670	(214) 938-8341

UTAH

Westminster College	Salt Lake City, UT 84105	(801) 488-4211

VERMONT

Castleton State College	Castleton, VT 05735	(802) 468-5611
Green Mountain College	Poultney, VT 05674	(802) 287-9313
Johnson State College	Johnson, VT 05656	(802) 635-2356
Lyndon State College	Lyndonville, VT 05851	(802) 626-9371
Coll. of St. Joseph the Provider	Rutland, VT 05701	(802) 773-5900
Trinity College of Vermont	Burlington, VT 05401	(802) 658-0337

VIRGINIA

Bluefield College	Bluefield, VA 24605	(703) 326-3682
Clinch Valley College	Wise, VA 24293	(703) 328-0217
Virginia Intermont College	Bristol, VA 24201	(703) 669-6101

WASHINGTON

Central Washington University	Ellensburg, WA 98926	(509) 963-1911
Evergreen State College	Olympia, WA 98505	(206) 866-6000
Pacific Lutheran University	Tacoma, WA 98447	(206) 535-7353
Saint Martin's College	Lacey, WA 98503	(206) 438-4372
Seattle Pacific University	Seattle, WA 98119	(206) 281-2085
Seattle University	Seattle, WA 98122	(206) 296-6400
University of Puget Sound	Tacoma, WA 98416-0710	(206) 756-3426
Western Washington University	Bellingham, WA 98225	(206) 676-3109
Whitman College	Walla Walla, WA 99362	(509) 527-5288
Whitworth College	Spokane, WA 99251-0002	(509) 466-3238

WEST VIRGINIA

Alderson-Broaddus College	Philippi, WV 26416	(304) 457-1700
Bluefield State College	Bluefield, WV 24701	(304) 327-4179
Concord College	Athens, WV 24712	(304) 384-5331
Davis and Elkins College	Elkins, WV 26241	(304) 636-1900
Fairmont State College	Fairmont, WV 26554	(304) 367-4220

Glenville State College	Glenville, WV 26351	(304) 462-7361
Salem-Teikyo University	Salem, WV 26426	(304) 782-5271
Shepherd College	Shepherdstown, WV 25443	(304) 876-2511
University of Charleston	Charleston, WV 25304	(304) 357-4820
West Liberty State College	West Liberty, WV 26074	(304) 336-8200
West Virginia State College	Institute, WV 25112	(304) 766-3140
West Virginia Institute of Tech.	Montgomery, WV 25136	(304) 442-3121
West Virginia Wesleyan College	Buckhannon, WV 26201	(304) 473-8099
Wheeling Jesuit College	Wheeling, WV 26003	(304) 243-2365

WISCONSIN

Cardinal Stritch College	Milwaukee, WI 53217	(414) 352-5400
Concordia University	Mequon, WI 53092-9652	(414) 243-5700
Edgewood College	Madison, WI 53711-1998	(608) 257-4861
Lakeland College	Sheboygan, WI 53082-0359	(414) 565-1239
Marian College of Fond du Lac	Fond du Lac, WI 54935	(414) 923-7625
Milwaukee School of Engineering	Milwaukee, WI 53201-0644	(414) 277-7230
Northland College	Ashland, WI 54806	(715) 682-1245
Viterbo College	LaCrosse, WI 54601	(608) 791-0391
University of Wisconsin	Eau Claire, WI 54702-4004	(715) 836-4183
University of Wisconsin	LaCrosse, WI 54601-9959	(608) 785-8616
University of Wisconsin/Parkside	Kenosha, WI 53141	(414) 553-2308
University of Wisconsin	River Falls, WI 54022-2568	(715) 425-3900
University of Wisconsin	Stevens Point, WI 54481	(715) 346-3888
University of Wisconsin/Stout	Menomonie, WI 54751	(715) 232-2116
Wisconsin Lutheran College	Milwaukee, WI 53226	(414) 774-0311

Appendix A
Sports Resume

Dr. Jeff Irving, an executive search consultant who works with professional resumes all the time, developed a sports resume using the same techniques. Study this model and note his suggestions:

- Put your name and social security number on every page.

- Be as concise as possible. Never use more than three well-spaced pages.

- Give a brief description of your high school.

- Put your academic credentials first, listing current courses, grade point average, test scores and any academic honors (always update this).

- List your sports experience, highlighting only the important things, including any national or regional honors and any meets, teams, camps, etc. outside school. Give all coaches' names, addresses and phone numbers. List your personal statistics and records, depending on your particular sport. For example, the model resume is for a rower, so the ergometer statistic is vitally important. Use reverse chronology, giving the most recent experience first, and limit the list to the last two years (keep this up to date as well).

- List other activities and interests, including any community work you may have done.

- Use good bright white stationery. Irving suggests 24-pound basis-weight paper with a 25 percent cotton content. This is not expensive or hard to find. Check out your local discount office supply store. Don't ruin your efforts with cheap paper.

- Write a cover letter, simply stating, for example, "I am a junior and member of the tennis team at W. R. Brown High School here in Anytown. I am very interested in learning more about Wossamotta U. and would appreciate any information you could send me . . ."

- *NOTE:* Do a first draft of your resume. Then set it aside for a week. Have you done a good job of highlighting your sports career? Does it really matter that you won the Fun Fair Derby in the fourth grade? Note in the model that Johnathon Doe lists only his rowing experience, although he is also a swimmer. Rowing is the sport he wants to take to college, so he concentrates on that. By simply listing swimming, he lets coaches know he has some versatility.

- When you have this resume together, keep it up to date and have copies with you on campus visits and for any communications with college personnel. You will want to give copies to your guidance counselors and coaches. Don't hesitate to ask for their help in drafting the resume, but take the responsibility to make a start. Don't expect them to do it for you.

SAMPLE SPORTS RESUME

RESUME

JONATHON HENRY DOE

SSN: 000-00-0000
345 Maple Drive
Anytown, USA 10000
(010) 123-4567

DATE OF GRADUATION: June, 1992

SECONDARY EDUCATION

Presently enrolled at W.R. Brown High School in Anytown, USA. W.R. Brown has a student body of approximately 1900 in grades 10 through 12.

GRADES AND TESTS

Present GPA: 3.5 of 4.0
Preliminary SAT: Verbal—90th percentile
                 Mathematics—74th percentile
                 (sophomore year results)

JUNIOR YEAR SUBJECTS

Advanced Placement Biology
American Civilization, honors English/History
French IV
Trigonometry/Elementary functions
Engineering Drawing

SPORTS

Crew: 8, 9, 10
Swimming: 9, 10

RECENT ROWING EXPERIENCE

Summer 1990:   Attended the Junior Men's Eastern Sculling Camp. (First experience with sculling.)

Anytown State Rowing Championships
Men's Junior Double—Bronze medal
(Rowed stroke, first sculling competition and first at 2000 meters.)
Coach: Mr. Irv Brown
         Tagmont Rowin Club
         Home: (010) 789-1011

Spring 1990:   Rowed 4 seat on the W. R. Brown Varsity Heavyweight Eight. (Only sophomore to make the boat.)

Regional Scholastic Rowing Association Championship Regatta. Varsity Heavyweight Eight—Gold Medal.

Loving Cup Regatta.
Varsity Heavyweight Eight—Bronze Medal.

Anytown Rowing Association Nationals.
Varsity Heavyweight Eight—Fourth Place.

Coach: Mr. C. Patrick Cooper
Head Coach
W. R. Brown High School
Office: (010) 121-3141
Home: (010) 516-1718

Fall 1989:   Rowed stroke in a Four with Coxswain made up of W.R. Brown rowers.

John Carlyle Memorial Regatta.
High School Four with Coxswain—Silver Medal.

Head of the Hunting Pond Regatta.
Championship Four with Coxswain—Fourth place.

Coach: Mr. Bob Young
Waterlovers Rowing Club
Home: (010) 192-0212
Office: (010) 223-2425

PERSONAL DATA

Date of Birth: November 22, 1973
Present Height: 6' 3"
Present Weight: 183 lbs.

2500 meter ergometer test: 8.33, taken in April, 1990.

75 lbs. bench pull/five minutes: 155 repetitions, taken in April, 1990.

—Format courtesy Jeffrey Irving Associates, Inc.

Appendix B
College Checklist

Coach Randy Lambert, athletic director and men's basketball coach at Maryville College, devised this checklist for high school coaches to use to keep track of their seniors. Individual student-athletes can easily use it, too. Unfortunately, it's not that hard to let something slip by undone. Individuals using this checklist may want to add lines for "sports resume sent" and "video sent," whenever applicable.

STEPS INVOLVED	PROSPECTIVE COLLEGES			
	A. _____	B. _____	C. _____	D. _____
I. Admission Process				
A. Application for Admission completed	_____	_____	_____	_____
B. High School transcript sent	_____	_____	_____	_____
C. National test scores sent	_____	_____	_____	_____
D. Campus visit made	_____	_____	_____	_____
E. Interviewed by college coach	_____	_____	_____	_____
II. Financial Aid Process				
A. Financial aid form sent for analysis	_____	_____	_____	_____
B. Results sent to College Financial Aid Office	_____	_____	_____	_____
C. Financial Aid package designed	_____	_____	_____	_____
D. Package accepted	_____	_____	_____	_____
E. Deposit for final commitment	_____	_____	_____	_____

Courtesy Coach Randy Lambert, Athletic Director, Maryville College